No Niche Necessary

How to build
a fulfilling multi-passionate business
by adding flavor in your unique way

Written By:
Kristen Leigh King

Silvester and Eve Publishing

For more information on the author, please go to:
www.kristenleighking.com

Silvester and Eve Publishing
4771 Bayou Blvd Suite 3 #111
Pensacola, Florida
www.silvesterandeve.com

Cover design and photography by Kristen Leigh King.

ISBN: 978-1-7336114-0-4

For permission, please contact the author at:
kristen@kristenleighking.com

Dedication

To my husband for listening to my ever-changing, crazy ideas and always believing that I'm capable of it all. I couldn't do any of this without you.

To my fellow military spouses working hard to hold together your families as well as build mobile, fulfilling careers. I see you, your determination and strength, and your incredible contribution.

This is for you.

Download your FREE audiobook of

No Niche Necessary

at:

www.kristenleighking.com/NoNicheNecessary-Audiobook

Table of Contents

No Niche Necessary

Introduction

You've decided that the typical career path just doesn't resonate with you, and you've made the conscious decision to try things your way. Whether you've already been trying out a bunch of different business ideas or you're still confused about why you can't figure out a niche and stick to it, it's probably time for some introspection in order to actually move forward.

I'm guessing you picked up this book knowing that the one-size-fits-all niche everyone tells you that you need is feeling a bit restrictive to you right about now. While there's definitely something to be said for those who can take one craft and hone it over years and decades of their lives, that just doesn't make sense for a lot of us.

If that sounds like something that's been playing in the back of your mind for awhile, then take heart. I'm going to share with you a whole new world that is available to you and can be established through your own choosing. A world where you drive the conversation based on your passions and strengths, and where you get to decide what fits and what doesn't. A scenario where being a business owner doesn't have to confine you but rather is an extension of your whole self and the talents you were meant to share with the world.

This isn't your typical career book. My flavor of inspiration is a bit of heartfelt compassion mixed with a strong drive to show you what's truly within yourself, in an attempt to open your eyes to who you are and the possibilities that come with it. You are different from everyone else. You are uniquely you and uniquely positioned to stand out as an impactful entrepreneur.

It just might not be in the way that you think or by conforming to the ideas you've been taught about what it means to create a successful business.

Here's the thing. I think you showed up here and picked up this book because the conventional business wisdom had you stuck and left you craving a new approach. Guess what?

That new approach lies in who you already are.

As a multi-passionate person, you've got the ability to create a whole new perspective around the way things are done in the world. By combining your zones of genius and the areas you excel in and by doing your best work, you can give people a much-needed breath of fresh air that allows them to see things in a way that wasn't apparent to them previously.

You have the ability to change minds, establish new experiences, innovate in stagnant areas, and lead movements. However, it has to start by recognizing your potential and understanding who you truly are at your core.

First and foremost, you are a combination of incredible strengths and latent potential. By putting yourself in the right frame of mind to embrace opportunities that merge with what's driving you at your core, you can be an unstoppable force.

It's time to stop thinking that you need to do business everyone else's way. It's time to take back control and realize who you are, many passions and all. And it's definitely time to be the one to decide how things are going to be in your own business.

Let this book serve you in two ways: first, as a starting point in your entrepreneurial journey to understand the power of being multi-passionate in a niche-centric world, and second to help you reframe your mindset around shaping your business into one that speaks to your whole soul and leaves you completely fulfilled.

This is not an easy done-for-you path, but it is one that will be fulfilling in the utmost of ways possible for you. So, decide to embrace all of who you are. Decide to put what's driving you front and center. Decide to unapologetically carve your own path that makes your soul full every single day.

Part One

Visualize Your Value

Chapter One

Creating Purpose in Your Life

College wasn't really all that fun for me. It's supposed to be the time of your life where you're partying all the time and doing all the things you won't be able to do later in life when you're more responsible. For me, that wasn't really how it happened. In all honesty, I think that while it was a hard time in my life, it was definitely a precursor to the idea that I was completely misaligned in my life.

I thought that I had chosen the perfect career path for myself. It was one that included the artistic aspects of my personality as I was going into architecture but was also structured as I chose Air Force Reserve Officers Training Corps (ROTC) to complement that. When I chose those areas to focus on, they felt like a good fit because I had already made up my mind that I was gonna work in a corporate office at some point and that I'd first be a leader and serve my country. Yet, the more I went through my courses and seasons at school, there was a shift for me. Something was no longer clicking, and I felt like everything had been taken off the rails even though I had planned it all so perfectly.

I started getting sick a lot. Not sleeping or eating much was pretty common because I was burning the candle at both ends pretty frequently. I would get up early and be at physical training for ROTC by six at the latest usually, and then I would stay up all night or at least the majority of the night working on my architecture projects. That was because the architecture projects were really big pushes that came at least every other week or so where we would essentially be designing an entire building in a few nights. Oh and by the way, you'd have to present it to a board of professors as well as your peers right after the deadline and be able to successfully illustrate the concept of your design and the reasoning behind all of the choices you made. So you would probably do all of that on about three hours of combined sleep over the course of two or three days.

Not to mention, those architecture projects usually sprang up at the most inopportune times for the rest of my schedule, including ROTC. The pressure and the intensity of that, while not ideal and definitely affecting my health, was never an excuse for me to keep pressing, though. I continued to push myself and drive through it as best I could, even though it was negatively impacting my performance on everything...my fitness tests, my designs, and my relationships. I just kept dismissing it and telling myself that I'd get over it.

Somehow, though, I managed to push my way to graduation, enter the Air Force as a civil engineering officer, and became a design and construction project manager. It wasn't until a little bit into this job that I started to understand what was wrong. While I loved being a project manager and serving my country as well as my community, I had this strong feeling that everything was out of alignment for me. That I needed to make some big changes, and that I needed to do something greater. I didn't know what that was, but I knew that the path I needed to take was different.

While I was unsure how that was going to play out for me at the moment, I resigned myself to just putting my head down and doing a good job at being a military officer in every way that I could at that point. I volunteered for as many leadership roles as I could, I pushed myself hard to be a good example at our fitness sessions, and I was extremely diligent about managing the construction projects I was in charge of seeing to completion. Even though I was crushing it in every area, I still felt the void.

It wasn't until there was a serious incident that our unit had to support and a strange, off-handed comment was made by one of my commanding officers that switched a light on inside of me. While we were in the process of working through this incident that occurred, he turned and asked me, "You don't like me very much, do you?"

While I was taken aback by the question and thought it was a very strange thing to ask, I knew at that moment I wasn't where I needed to be. That while I may have needed to go through this experience or learn something from that job or the people I worked with, I realized that it wasn't the path I was meant to be on for very long.

It was a clarifying moment that essentially became a catalyst for me taking action after that. Since I had now realized that I didn't want to become the person that I was supposed to be looking up to or the person stuck in that job as my career, I started thinking about what was possible. If not this, then what?

When the opportunity came, I jumped. One day I found out that there were a few spots available in my career field to voluntarily separate from the military because there was an overage of officers. It meant that if chosen, the Air Force would thank you for your service and tell you that you had completed your commitment to them. There were only five slots for my group at the time across the entire branch of service for my career field, but I knew immediately that one of those was meant for me.

I went home, talked it over with my husband, and decided to just do it. I walked into my commander's office the next day to tell him I was putting my paperwork in, and he immediately told me there was a slot to be filled for deployment, and it would most likely go to me. At that point there were a lot of mixed emotions about it all. Deployment was what I had always trained to do. It was part of my job as a military officer to serve when needed and was something that I had been gearing up to do for the previous years.

But it didn't feel right to me.

It didn't feel like that was the best way for me to serve my purpose because I had already come to the realization that there was a different path for me. So while I accepted the assignment and prepared to represent my unit on that upcoming deployment, I also went ahead and filed my paperwork to separate. At that point, I knew I had to try. I had to at least see what came of it because I felt so strongly that one of those separation spots was meant for me.

Several weeks later when I finally received a response back about my paperwork, I found out that had been denied. I got denied. As I heard my commander saying it to me, all I could focus on was him smiling. You know how people tend to smile sometimes when they give bad news as if to soften the blow? It was that kind of a smile, and it stung.

I graciously told him that I understood, would review the response, and continue preparing for the deployment. After I had gone back through the paperwork, though, I realized that it was done incorrectly. That it had been filed under the wrong category and thus rejected because it didn't fit the requirements. I immediately knew that I had to do it again. That wasn't the end of it, and that there was still a spot open just for me.

I went back to my commander, told him about the inaccuracies, and what needed to happen to make it right. After getting him onboard with trying it again, I pushed it through one more time with the knowledge that there was only one lingering spot left for my year group...one overage spot that was still needed to put my career field back in line with its correct personnel numbers. I believed to my very core at that moment that it was still mine.

And you know what? This time it came back approved.

Having conviction in yourself is not completely contingent on knowing what you want or need to do. Sometimes it's just about the mere idea that you trust yourself above all else. I knew that I was capable of something so much bigger than what I was doing in my immediate circumstances. It wasn't because I didn't believe in being a military officer, my ability to make a difference, or in the ways I was helping as a project manager. I just had conviction in knowing that something else was waiting for me, and it was up to me to go after it.

I had one day to pack up my office, out-process the entire military, and move on. One single day was it. It was so quick that I didn't have time to truly process the fact. I just remember that once the day was over and I was driving back home, Tom Petty's *Free Fallin'* song came on the radio. It was just like in the *Jerry McGuire* movie after he quits his job without a backup plan. At that moment, as I sang along without a plan of my own, I felt the most free that I've ever felt in my life. The most free, energized, and empowered that I had felt before. And no matter what was coming, I was ready.

So my point with this story is to share with you that it's okay to not know the one true path for you. It's okay to not have that thing you've always known in your heart you were gonna be when you grew up. It's okay to try different things and have nothing stick. But just know that having conviction in yourself and your capabilities, no matter how widespread or scattered they may seem, is all it takes to build a life of purpose.

The fact that you're waking up to the idea that you no longer want to live a life based on someone else's priorities and create your own path that truly speaks to who you are is a powerful thing. It doesn't have to be something you've been dreaming about for years and years. It could just be a nagging feeling that you're meant for something more and to make an impact in some way, shape, or form that's not totally clear yet.

I'm here to tell you that in all likelihood if you're here reading this book, it's because it's not just one thing that's calling you. It's a path. One that you carve for yourself based on your many strengths, abilities, and passions. It's an approach to life that allows you to authentically shine your light on the world in your own unique way as you discover and combine the things that truly make your soul full.

Living with regret is a hard pill to swallow, and it's one that you have the ability right now to reject. If you've been living with the idea that you just need to choose one career and stick to it in order to be successful, then let me be the first to tell you that that approach to building a fruitful life is antiquated and keeping you stuck. You have the power to create a life and business that you love and doesn't constrain or confine you.

We're living in an age where many people are finally waking up to the fact that they are in control and can create their own realities. This generation of millennials is a generation of idealists that refuse to take on the traditional nine-to-five jobs working for someone else's priorities just because they were told that's what you need to do to be successful. People are throwing the idea of having one sole focus back in the faces of those who try to put them into a box and tell them that putting your head down to focus on only one thing is what it takes to get ahead.

A new renaissance is coming. For those of us who feel like we were never meant to do just one thing, it's a breath of fresh air. As this new generation grows up and starts taking on jobs and building businesses of their own, there's a convergence happening in our society. One of free-thinking idealists combined with the movement of authenticity in business and branding. It's an exciting time where people are much more interested in doing business with other real people rather than faceless companies that don't connect with them on an emotional level.

You can see it all over social media as you interact with others. There's been a massive shift from the polished photographs and carefully curated feeds to a more genuine inside look into people's real lives and stories. That authenticity is building the true know, like, and trust factor highly coveted in entrepreneurship circles and those wanting to gain followers for their businesses. And it's all based around showing up as who you really are, in every aspect of yourself.

Forget about having one business tailored explicitly to one service and another business or profile tailored to something else. You are what you're selling. If you're niching down so much that people can't see all of who you are, then it's like putting blinders on your audience and reducing their ability to see what's so great and different about you.

Here's the good news. You aren't one-dimensional. You never have been. Maybe you've found yourself wandering from one interest to the next, trying out many different things, and at some point getting to a place where you feel bored or satisfied enough with it that you need to move on. People may have told you that you're just lost or confused and haven't found that one right thing for you yet. Perhaps you've already been planning to start your own business, but you just can't decide on a specific niche because you have so many ideas and interests.

You're not alone. You've got a plethora of unique talents and gifts all in the right combination just for you. See, some people approach the world by honing in on just one thing and being great at it. Then there are those of us who are multi-passionate. We're the jacks-of-all-trades who are developing a lifetime of learning to be proficient enough in a wide variety of areas that when combined create a new and different approach. A unique approach to things that the world absolutely needs and wouldn't have if not for your unique combination of strengths and talents.

If you're just realizing that you may fall into this category, then take comfort in the fact that the recognition of the significant place that multi-passionate people hold in our society is gaining momentum. Coupled with the emergence of this new generation of idealists and authentic communication, we can establish a new paradigm for not only our careers but for the way we view entrepreneurship as well.

This is the new renaissance, and it's starting with multi-passionate people just like you.

I'm sure you've recognized by now that you're not a one-dimensional person and that you approach life differently than most. There isn't just one thing that stands out to you that you're really good at above all else. You've developed so many different interests and are constantly drawn to learning about new things or exploring different passions all the time. There's never a time where you really just settle on one thing for long until you're back to exploring something new.

These are your genius zones, and as a multi-passionate person, you have many. Now, I know that everyone has a lot of passions and interests that they dabble in throughout their lives. However, not everyone has the same propensity to broadly learn, explore, and quickly pick up those interests and skills in the way that we're discussing here. In her TEDtalk, writer, author, and community leader, Emilie Wapnick, calls this being a multi-potentialite, and she celebrates the ability of multi-potentialites to intertwine their many abilities to create a new perspective.[1] Margaret Lobenstine refers to this as being a "Renaissance Soul" where you have a dynamic curiosity about the world and an incredible yearning for new and different things that feed your soul.[2] Marie Forleo coined the term "multi-passionate" to describe the ability to pursue many interest areas that converge together to create a unique perspective and value in the world.[3]

When I use the term "multi-passionate," I'm talking about the very specific approach to life that all of these women have addressed. It's an approach in which you shine a light on your many capabilities and talents, and you are constantly moving back and forth between those genius zones. You get your energy and fuel your soul by pursuing something for a set period of time, and then it's almost as if an internal alarm clock goes off and tells you that you've done enough to be satisfied with that one interest. So it's time to move on to the next.

In this way, it's almost like being introverted or extroverted. Your innate approach to life is how you best get energized from what you pursue. There's nothing wrong

---

[1] https://www.ted.com/talks/ emilie_wapnick_why_some_of_us_don_t_have_one_true_calli ng?language=en
[2] https://www.goodreads.com/book/show/ 415595.The_Renaissance_Soul
[3] https://www.businessinsider.com/business-coach-marie-forleo-career-advice-2018-8

with being one way or the other, either great at one thing or a jack-of-all-trades. Our society needs both for different purposes. The problem lies in our own ability to accept ourselves for who we truly are, break free from the conventional wisdom of our society, and embrace your innate approach to life.

You've got a lot of things to bring to the table in terms of your strengths and that allows you to combine them and establish a new perspective on the world. One that is truly needed by many people, and if you were to listen to the conventional wisdom of putting yourself into just one chosen box or niche, it would be a disservice to us all.

Let me just say right now that this is a gift and not a curse. If you've considered becoming an entrepreneur and starting your own business, but the fact that you have so many different interests is holding you back, then I want to tell you a secret: Being multi-passionate is the true essence of an entrepreneur.

You have to carve your own path instead of taking a specific one that's already been laid out for you. You have to seize a variety of different opportunities that come your way in order to make a difference. You need to see the big picture and bring a wide breadth of knowledge into everything you do to make something truly new and innovative. Above all else, you need to trust that your gut will guide you as you follow what feels right to you and what speaks to you the most.

Being an entrepreneur is about all of these things, and you just so happen to be innately wired to do just that. So just because the conventional wisdom may have been that you'll succeed when you focus on one thing and only ever do that one kind of work, it doesn't mean that you can't turn that way of thinking on its head and reframe the way you approach it for yourself.

The idea of that may seem risky right now, and you may be totally unsure of whether that's going to work because you've been trained to think that it won't for so long. Let me just reassure you, though, that it's about reshaping your perspective to understand how you can best thrive as an entrepreneur.

You are in control here. You may be currently floundering between different business ideas, but you know that you really do want to live life on your own terms and make it work as your own boss. If you're not sure how to choose a direction or what that even means for you, just know that you don't have to settle or be resigned to someone else's idea of what business-building entails.

You've got real value in your many ideas, passions, and pursuits. The fact that you have so many things you love and bring into your life demonstrates the incredible potential for you to be an innovator in your own way. We need more people like you for our society to grow and evolve, and I want you to feel empowered by your ability to make a real impact in your own way.

You get to decide if the traditional way of doing business and building a career is right for you or not. As you venture out on your own (which I'm so excited for you to do), I want you to always carry with you the knowledge that you create your own reality. This is your journey and your life. No one else's but your own. The choices you make to shape it are yours alone. I'm here to be the guiding light showing you the many possibilities that lie within yourself. Your ability to embrace and combine your unique passions is the key factor in getting your purpose out into the world effectively and creating a life of purpose and fulfillment.

Do you really think you're ever gonna be fulfilled by just one thing? If you do, then maybe you are just being indecisive at this point. But I think you know better. I think you know deep down that you're always going to be pulled in several different directions, and that's not a bad thing. It's what lights you up and fuels you to keep going. So stop right now with feeling less than because someone told you that you're indecisive or confused. Stop feeling stuck because you can't choose a business niche and move forward. It's time to get comfortable with who you really are and your approach to life.

This is just the beginning for you to open yourself up and understand that you really can create a fulfilling business that speaks to every part of who you are and allows you the freedom to explore whatever fuels your soul. All it's going to take is the ability to listen to your gut, be courageous enough to be who you truly are, and to decide that you'll no longer conform to the limits that everyone else has arbitrarily put on you. I know you're capable of that. Do you?

Chapter Two

Beyond Conventional Wisdom

Can we talk for a minute about our culture? Every culture in the world is different and approaches work life differently. In the Western world, especially in the United States, we value a chosen career path that we often think defines us. Think about when you go to parties or events and introduce yourself to someone new. I bet nine times out of ten they ask what you do for a living and expect to receive a very standard one or two-word answer. This isn't necessarily the case in other countries where they instead ask how things are going in your life or what you do for fun.[4]

It just reiterates how ingrained having one career path is in our society. So much so, that it's now permeated over to the entrepreneurship world where the experts will tell

---

[4] https://www.businessinsider.com/american-customs-that-are-offensive-abroad-2015-8

you that to be successful, a particular niche is necessary. Ask anyone giving out business advice these days, and they'll reiterate that you've got to do one thing really well for a long time to get known. Then, you'll be the go-to person for that one thing.

Before we dive into why all the advice is being presented this way, let's clarify the differences between the terms career, small business, and entrepreneurship. In terms of having a career, I'm talking about that lifelong calling that we're all supposed to have according to society. You know it all too well from growing up thinking about what you wanted to be and having to decide your major in college. Running a business is just one potential avenue in your career, and it's highly likely that if you're still reading, this is your intention. To run your own business means that you're deciding that you want to take a major role in the operations, management, and leadership of a company. It means that you're willing to be your own boss, possibly be in charge of other employees or contractors, and provide the means to support yourself and those people financially. Plus, in terms of the basic foundation of running a small business, it generally means offering a product or service to a very specific market. Thus, as a business owner, you have a "great deal of responsibility as well as a great feeling of achievement and freedom that is never realized by those who work for someone else."[5]

---

[5] https://www.entrepreneurmag.co.za/advice/starting-a-business/launch/what-it-means-to-own-your-own-business/

Now, let's clarify the distinction between running a small business and being an entrepreneur. An entrepreneur is someone who carves their own path in business, seizing opportunities as they come, or taking on a variety of projects or work as part of their ongoing entrepreneurial journey. Separate from a small business, an entrepreneur is usually more widely versed in several areas and thus chooses to broaden their reach on the work they undertake. "Entrepreneurs and business owners have a different relationship with their companies. Entrepreneurs view their companies as assets. Something to be developed, shaped and readied for market. And then sold for a profit so that they can move on to the next "Big One."[6] This is the important factor that's being blurred quite heavily these days and is part of the underlying problem of why the advantages of multi-passionate people in business are being marginalized.

To be successful in business, entrepreneurship is being looked at through the same lens as running a small business, but they are distinct and separate. Many people who actually are working hard to start up and run a small business are calling themselves entrepreneurs rather than small business owners. While it's an incredible achievement to take charge of your life and build

---

[6] https://www.forbes.com/sites/quickerbettertech/2012/06/06/the-difference-between-an-entrepreneur-and-a-small-business-owner/#229eda7a6635

your own future in any capacity, there should be more of a clear understanding about the difference between the two...especially because we're trying to shove everyone into this category of entrepreneurship when personalities don't always align to it. Some are meant to be specialists while others are meant to be jacks-of-all-trades. Neither is better than the other, but telling them both to approach business-building in the same way is not feasible.

In my own life, knowing I wanted to be an entrepreneur for a long time, I listened to the prevailing talk about how there was one specific thing out there I needed to do rather than taking stock of what I actually had to contribute to society in my own unique way. I thought that all I needed to do was test out a few different ideas and find that one thing I'd be really good at and focus on it to continue growing my business forever. The problem was that I was conflating the niching down of being a small business owner with the idea of being a successful entrepreneur. I had heard the two used interchangeably for so long that in my mind, the approach to doing both became somewhat synonymous. So I literally tried everything to find that one right niche for myself instead of recognizing my innate propensity to have a broad range of work.

Initially when I stopped doing project management, I thought I'd be a real estate developer. I even went as far as to register my limited liability company, get a business partner, and get quotes from local contractors for a potential project. Then the constraints of that venture set in, and I felt a bit boxed in. I knew that it wasn't sustainable for our life as a military family moving around, and that I wouldn't be willing to stick with it over a distance. So that idea was scrapped.

After going back to school for awhile and getting certifications and degrees in everything from environmental design to community development, I got the itch again to try my hand at entrepreneurship. But I was still listening to those voices telling me that there was one thing I needed to be good at and stick to long-term. So I opened my handmade business and designed party supplies and invitations while we lived overseas. After awhile, though, the internal multi-passionate clock started ticking once more.

I tried event planning as I volunteered for a few nonprofit organizations. I tried blogging about sustainable living, travel and living overseas, and food. Once I got into the food blogging, I started to think maybe I could actually find my niche. The more I blogged, the more I knew that I wasn't getting traffic and needed to make some improvements. That's when I started learning photography, and it started actually taking off for me.

I took photography courses, went on retreats, immersed myself in food photography, product photography, and then eventually portrait photography. The better I got, the more I upped my game because I thought that was going to be the big thing for me. I started working with small business owners to take their headshots and create videos for their brands. And while it was fun and rewarding to celebrate all of those people I got to work with, I felt the itch to move on big time.

I knew that I still had so much to give beyond taking photos. I moved into the coaching arena where I started helping those same business owners improve their visual branding and connect more with their audiences. As I moved closer to coaching, I started to put more of my passions to use and combine them together into something fruitful. That's when I started to realize that doing that actually made me a whole lot happier than I had been chasing any specific niche before, and I was connecting more with the people who actually needed my work.

But I didn't stop there. I realized that I was never going to be fully happy doing just one thing. That while I loved photography and was on the road to building a profitable business, my internal clock was destined to go off again, leaving me wanting more. And of course, it did.

This time, though, I dug deep into why it was actually happening. I knew that I was a multi-passionate person at this point, but now I had the knowledge and ability to piece together what would be a complete overhaul of how I approached being an entrepreneur...an entrepreneur and not just a single-focused small business owner. I realized that I had been playing by everyone else's rules when those rules were not created with the understanding of a multi-passionate person or how that type of person fits into the business mold.

I now understood that while focus is essential to growing a business, the way business is being taught to us as multi-passionate people is doing us a huge disservice. Because of that, society is missing out on a wealth of knowledge, insight, and innovation as we are being stove-piped into one idea of what it means to build a business. So while understanding business in terms of having one niche can be extremely valid, as it's been tested countless times over, the framing of it suggests that you need to be a specific type of person to be successful. That the type of person who can focus on one thing for years or decades to perfect their craft will be the most successful. Quite frankly, that myopic idea categorizes everyone in business as having the same mindset and approach to doing things. For many of us that's completely inconsistent with the way we approach life. We are not all built to do one thing for years and years, and our world is better because of it.

So why on earth would we tell people that if they wanted to build a successful career and business, that they had to do it in one particular way that would confine them and constrain them? Why would we tell people to limit themselves? And why on earth would we think that would help us improve our society by being a group of solely one-dimensional people? It's not right.

There's a place in our society and in the business world as well for all kinds of people including those that need to specialize and those who are the jacks-of-all-trades. And because we are all different, we shouldn't be teaching business in the same way to everyone. So what's needed is a reframe of the problem and a new perspective of how to solve it.

For those of us that know deep down that we are meant to build something of our own and start a business, we must realize that it is possible to be successful no matter what our propensity to approaching life. Being multi-passionate means that you have incredible potential in business, and you should never let anyone tell you otherwise. It just so happens that you sway more toward the entrepreneurship side of things rather than being a typical small business owner with a clear, specific inclination. In your case, entrepreneurship is ideal because you're not afraid to venture in different directions and do things unconventionally.

Just because the lines of having a single-focus small business and being an entrepreneur have been blurred in many circles, doesn't mean that you need to believe it. Just because you're being taught that niching down means you've gotta choose only one thing to do forever in order to be successful, doesn't mean you need to convince yourself of that either. Each individual project or endeavor you undertake may actually have its own niche. However, the focus you have as a multi-passionate entrepreneur can actually depend upon a theme that connects all of the things you do. If you think about it that way, you'll be able to reframe the typical idea of a niche into something that actually suits your multi-passionate perspective more appropriately.

Giving yourself a broader theme to base your multitude of work around can feel a lot more manageable and freeing than having to stare down one tiny little business niche for the rest of your working years. Instead, this idea leaves you open enough to explore everything that makes you feel fulfilled. It allows you to be authentic to yourself and to quit cramming your skills and capabilities into a business framework that other people have created. You can build your own framework, and I'll show you how.

Before we go into the specifics of how you actually do all of that, let's go back to the so-called experts for a bit more. When a lot of coaches or people teaching business see you as a multi-passionate person, they don't fully comprehend that you approach life inherently differently. Because of this, they won't fully know how to teach you differently because they think you're just being indecisive. As I'll explain, this is completely untrue for those of us who are naturally multi-passionate. Right now, though, I want you to be aware of this fact as you dive into the entrepreneurial world and hear so many people saying that being multi-passionate is an excuse for not sticking to anything. It's their flaw for not educating themselves enough to help you, rather than the other way around.

The experts should be the ones who have the ability to frame things in a way that people understand them better. After all, that's what teachers do with their students who are all different, right? But something happened along the way where the method of teaching was no longer being adjusted to suit the student's best learning needs, and now that has been to the detriment of innovation in our society.

You are not flawed. Our system is flawed in approaching business and entrepreneurship from one very specific perspective. Don't for one second buy into it. You can do better and be the entrepreneur you know that you are by adjusting your mindset and looking at how to build a successful business in a new way. That way starts with you looking inward and knowing to your very core that there is something driving everything within you, and that it all needs to be shared in the world in your unique way.

Once you've moved past the conventional wisdom telling you to niche down to do one specific thing, you then need to reframe your mindset around how you have a built-in ability to stand out in a crowded marketplace as a multi-passionate entrepreneur. While everyone else is preaching about how to market yourself to stand out even though they've just told you to be as focused and generic as possible, this is where you've got your biggest advantage.

People are no longer interested in doing business with one-dimensional, faceless companies. Consumers are craving real connection and would much rather get what they need from someone who genuinely connects with them over a company who's far from having an authentic connection with them at all. People are choosing individual influencers online and micro-influencers with small followings on social media or their blogs because they're authentically showing up in unconventional ways. Those are the ones who are resonating with the people who need them the most and who are making the biggest impact on people's lives through relationship-building.

The basis of this lies in building what's called your "know, like, and trust factor." This refers to the fact that before people buy from you, they first need to get to know who you are, like you and click with you, and then trust that you can, in fact, help them or provide them with value.[7] Without these three things, there most likely won't be anyone buying what you're selling. It's not the product or service alone that sells. It always comes back to how it resonates with the person and

---

[7] https://www.bizjournals.com/bizjournals/how-to/marketing/2016/08/know-like-and-trust-the-essence-of-networking.html

whether there's an underlying connection made in order to emotionally charge them in the direction of buying.

Now, if you are authentic as you share your story and spread your talents and expertise in your unique way, you will be able to truly connect much faster than if you were to put your head down and only try to do one thing all the time. You still have a message to share through your work just as the single-focused business owner has one thing that they do, but it's all in the way you position yourself. And when you have a very distinctive positioning based on combining several areas you're passionate about, the people who click with you are going to choose you over someone else every day of the week.

Building that relationship and clicking with your ideal audience is going to be something that you do really well because you'll inherently attract the right people to your message. Through your distinct approach and combination of your personality, skills, and value you provide, your tribe will start to get to know you, like you, and trust you as someone just like them...someone who understands them and whose perspective is just the right flavor for what they need and want. So doing that one specific thing may seem like advice that you need to follow because it's tried-and-true, but in the context of standing out from the crowd and getting people to really know who you are, showing up with everything that you are wins hands down.

Along with having the ability to resonate with people comes the opportunity to create an experience that they won't forget. Think about the reasoning behind why people refer their friends to someone or something. Usually, it has nothing to do with the actual product or service that they're getting but more so about how they felt and the experience they got out of the process. We do this a lot in our daily lives for recommending great restaurants or movies to friends. If you found a great Italian restaurant in town that had a romantic ambiance and they made every course of the meal special by presenting it well, then you're probably more likely to recommend that place over the five other Italian restaurants in town that don't offer an experience like that.

Let's take the movies you love and recommend to others. Chances are that you had a great experience of being fully immersed in the movie and were emotionally drawn to it somehow. So the likelihood of recommending it to someone else is that much higher because it gave you an experience you won't forget. The same is true in our business endeavors. If we offer the same product or service as everyone else with no flavor, no presentation, no spark, then chances are it'll just be categorized as all the others doing the same exact thing. However, if we take the time to really develop a full experience that someone will never forget and will be totally different from what your customers would get elsewhere, then you're onto something special.

The key point here is that you have the chance to create a significant emotional connection with your audience and customers not only by building your know, like, and trust factor but by also immersing them in an experience unlike any other. Working with you should feel like a new world has opened up to them due to the unique take you have on a product or service that is usually commonplace. It should be something that plays to your strengths, blends your many passions to create a new twist, and allows you to put your offer in a totally different context that's a welcome breath of fresh air.

I want you to think about the deliverables in your business as the culmination of an innovative, creative journey that your ideal audience is taken on...one where you share your broader perspective to give a unique way of solving a problem or creating change. Think about creating solutions by piecing together the multitude of knowledge and expertise areas you have or by merging areas that you know would compliment each other in order to stand out from the crowd. You want to be more than just a business owner who delivers a product. You want to be the one who makes people think differently, feel entertained, or stir up a big emotion that they're yearning for at their core. By highlighting your multidimensionality in your work, you can do all of those things as a successful entrepreneur.

Let me give you an example of how you could possibly do this. Let's say you love to focus on helping moms improve their health. That may mean that the main focus of your business is a primary passion of yours for teaching yoga, but you know that you want to incorporate your many passions into the business and create an experience for your customers. In order to do this, you may choose to host an in-person retreat where you teach yoga sessions, but you're not going to stop there. When attendees arrive at your retreat, they're greeted with a welcome basket full of family-friendly exercise equipment and a cookbook for meal planning. As you take your attendees through your retreat, you also add in ways for them to send photos back to their kids about how they're getting healthy or maybe you even include a trip to the local farmer's market where you shop for fresh produce to snack on in between yoga sessions. Then, at the end of the retreat, you present a special video that you've been compiling throughout the retreat to celebrate the transformation that has occurred.

Do you see how that can be an incredible experience for someone to remember and one that they can't wait to share with their friends? All because instead of deciding you were just going to teach another yoga class like everyone else, you've managed to incorporate your other passions of healthy cooking, parenting, and even videography to create a meaningful and impactful approach to what you do. I don't know about you, but if I had the choice of going to this retreat or a standard, recurring yoga course, I would choose the one that gave me an experience I'd never forget.

That's just one example of how you can use your multi-passionate capabilities to make an impact through your business. No one is going to be able to provide the same experience or outlook that you can, so developing your business plan around several passions can actually be a pretty incredible advantage. Why not use that? There are so many entrepreneurs these days who are missing the mark in this department because they've got blinders on to seeing only the output of their work. But when you look at the bigger picture of solving people's pain points and delivering your value through a unique experience, that's when the real magic happens.

As we go further into the specifics of developing a business framework, I'll explain more about creating this customer experience and playing up your many passions through your offers. For now, I want you to recognize that the experience you create helps you to resonate more fully with customers and allow them to become loyal, raving fans just by working with you in your unique way.

You may think that it's great in theory to bring several of your passions together and know a little about a lot of things. However, don't you really just need expertise in something to help someone with their problems? In most cases, the answer is actually no. I bet with the things you're passionate about and have studied or learned, you've gained at least 60-70%, if not more, of the information or skill you need to help someone. Chances are you've immersed yourself in those areas for a while, up until the point you were satisfied that you knew enough of it to be helpful.

In fact, the widespread idea of doing 10,000 hours of work in a subject to master it has been misrepresented.[8] In actuality, the original study conducted by Anders Ericcson at Florida State University established that the 10,000 hours was an average value, and that there was no magic number attributed to mastery. It's the quality of the hours spent learning a subject that really plays a significant role in attaining mastery. Another study done by the *Intelligence* journal reported that practice may only be responsible for as little as 12% of mastery and factors such as genetics may contribute as well. Also building upon these inconsistencies to the 10,000-hour rule, entrepreneurs such as Tim Ferriss are now supporting the idea that it is possible to be skilled in many different areas without devoting a lifetime to each craft. Ferriss rallies his followers with the idea that you can quickly master any subject with the right mindset and approach, and because of this philosophy he has

---

[8] Nightingale, Rob. (2015, December 9). "The 10,000 Hour Rule is Wrong. How to Really Master a Skill." Retrieved from https://www.makeuseof.com/tag/10000-hour-rule-wrong-really-master-skill/

amassed a significant following of those who see the value in his thinking.[9]

Most likely as you've developed your interests and skills over the years there has been something inside you telling you when you were proficient enough in each subject. You've trusted your instincts enough to solidly say that you could help someone or teach someone with your knowledge. So for you to know at least 60-70% of the general knowledge on a subject, and probably a good amount of specific knowledge, too, you'll be able to help a massive amount of people with that knowledge alone. For those who are struggling significantly with a problem and need that top 30% of extremely detailed knowledge into a subject, they can always seek out someone who excels in that single focus area. You, however, with your 60-70% of general learned knowledge on several subjects, have the capability to help the vast majority of people needing help in those areas.

Basically, what I'm saying here is that you've learned about the things you're passionate about in order to have 60% more knowledge on the subject than most people, and that's significant. Plus, I'm willing to bet that you've got closer to 80% of knowledge in at least one or two areas that can serve as your primary

---

[9] Nightingale, Rob. (2015, December 9). "The 10,000 Hour Rule is Wrong. How to Really Master a Skill." Retrieved from https://www.makeuseof.com/tag/10000-hour-rule-wrong-really-master-skill/

strengths to focus your business around. We'll discuss this in more detail later, but I want to touch on it here to get you started in framing your mindset around your primary strengths.

Now, think about coupling that percentage of knowledge in a certain subject with other areas that you're passionate about. You're now giving yourself the ability to think outside the box as you present your ideas, formulate solutions, and create that customer experience all from combining expertise in different subjects. This will give you a huge advantage as you no longer will be competing with others. No one else will have the exact same combination of skills, experiences, and abilities that you do or who can put them together into a complete knowledge base the way you can for your customers. Talk about an incredible realization in how being a multi-passionate person can actually fuel your success!

Whenever I work with people on design or branding projects, the one thing I always tell them is to draw upon ideas from other industries. Whether their business is in handmade products, fashion styling, or architecture, the key to tapping into their creative genius, getting out of a creative rut, and creating something extraordinary always lies in looking beyond what's right in front of you. Think about how it feels to stare at a computer screen all day long. Your eyes need an adjustment, your body needs to move and change positions, and you just need some fresh air or sunshine a lot of times. That's because altering our perspective from doing one thing for too long is incredibly rejuvenating.

The same goes for your creative genius. A big advantage you have as a multi-passionate person is that you have inspiration coming at you from many different angles. If you allow yourself to fully explore what interests you and be guided by what moves your soul, you will be inspired. Whereas if you decide to box yourself in and only focus on one tiny little niche, you may as well be stifling your growth just by limiting your ideas and ability to bring new concepts into your work. Creativity needs to come from somewhere. Tapping into several different areas of interest will give you the benefit of processing things with an open mind, finding ways of doing things that one industry does really well over another, and getting a lot more light bulb moments when you come across an interesting approach that can be applied to a completely different subject.

As we've talked about before, multi-passionate people don't put themselves in bubbles. You explore, learn, and express yourself best through the integration of several areas, not just one. So whether you're currently focusing on a photography project or a writing project, you could still gain inspiration by taking the time to study your other interests in areas such as cooking, travel, or even sports. What's more, this method of looking outside of one industry for inspiration from others is a surefire way to encourage growth. As someone aspiring to be an

entrepreneur and make an impact, growth is pretty
much non-negotiable when it comes to getting your
message out to as many people as possible.

Let me go one step further with this and say that exploring more areas than one will allow you to fill up your
own multi-passionate well. When you get bored or need
something more stimulating to reset your attention,
inspiration, and passion, it's most likely because you've
let your well run dry. You've got to keep your well full to
generate new perspectives, feel fulfilled, and really shine
as you live your purpose through your talents. If your
well runs dry and you've got nothing left to give or you
feel incredibly stuck, chances are that you haven't allowed yourself to fully explore the things that have been
calling your soul. If you give yourself the opportunity to
find inspiration in many areas regularly or build them
into a business strategy where you can utilize tangential
passions and interests, you'll be able to keep that multi-
passionate well full for much longer.

As you keep your multi-passionate well full and seek
inspiration from several subjects and industries, you'll
be able to piece together bits of expertise here and there,
combine them with your experience, and generate a
genius way of approaching whatever you're working on
at the moment. Just to give you an idea of how a company has made a massive impact on the world by pulling
ideas from several passions, take a look at Apple Computers. Steve Jobs forged a vision for the way people
would one day use computers in their daily lives and

what that would actually look like.[10] He drew inspiration from calligraphy, user interface design, psychology, minimalist living, technology, and many other subjects. Once Steve was able to find the intersection of his ideas and pull bits and pieces together from each one of his passions, he was able to dictate an incredible change in our society.[11]

This sparked a massive consumer movement and a whole new way of looking at how technology could be used by individuals all because he was willing to look at it through the lens of multiple different knowledge bases and combine the parts of each that made sense. It may not seem like it right now, but you as a multi-passionate person have the ability to do this as well. Maybe not on the same grand scale as Apple, unless that's your goal, but it is quite possible for you to achieve the same interdisciplinary impact all from combining your various knowledge areas and allowing yourself to tap into that creative genius.

How would it feel if you were to impact even a tiny fraction of the lives that Steve Jobs did all because you were to fully embrace being a jack-of-all-trades and see how different disciplines can shape one another? What incredible changes would you be able to make in the

---

[10] Isaacson, Walter. *Steve Jobs*. https://www.amazon.com/Steve-Jobs-Walter-Isaacson/dp/1451648537

[11] Isaacson, Walter. *Steve Jobs*. https://www.amazon.com/Steve-Jobs-Walter-Isaacson/dp/1451648537

world even on a small scale if you just interpreted things a little bit differently or altered the concept of something a little bit based on other skill sets you may have? Wouldn't it be worth it to know that all of your passions, skills, and talents are purposeful and meaningful in the exact way that they've been given to you?

Give yourself a moment to really sit with that thought and recognize now what it would mean to you if you fully embraced everything that you're capable of instead of boxing yourself in or holding yourself back. Feel how it would actually feel to bring about a change in our society or impact someone's life. Visualize yourself doing the work, presenting the ideas and solutions, and realizing your full potential. It's a powerful thing, and when you can finally see it in your own mind, you can start to create it in the world.

To wrap up our discussion of moving past the conventional wisdom, I want to reiterate that the best course of action is being real with yourself. You ultimately have to be willing to choose your own inner compass over what everyone else is telling you will work. At the end of the day, all the business coaches and expert advice isn't necessarily the best thing for what's inside of you needing to come out or the path that you need to take. This is your journey, and no one else but you can determine if you're going in the right direction.

Stepping out of your comfort zone to take chances or to try out different things takes courage. If you're willing to take the first steps and acknowledge that you're meant for an unconventional life, then that's all you need in the beginning to get you moving forward. You're going to have to push passed the conformist ideas and things you've been taught to get to what makes sense for your own work. You'll get there one step at a time, though, and the path will become clearer and clearer the more you listen to your gut and take action.

In the coming chapters, I'll show you how to hone in on what you do in an authentic way, but you have to know that being successful ultimately starts with you. You must know yourself, trust your gut, and not allow anyone including yourself to put limits on what you can do. Your career, business, and entrepreneurship journey belong to you and within that so does your story and driving message. Every single day, ask yourself, "Am I willing to show up as the leader and innovator I'm meant to be?" Then, step into your genius zones and own them.

Chapter Three

Removing What's Holding You Back

Everyone has blocks, and as a multi-passionate entrepreneur, you're bound to have quite a few as well. That's why I want to address those here before we move further into building a business framework. If you have any fears that you're carrying with you now, chances are they'll follow you moving forward. That means you'll just hold yourself back a little further down the road, and we don't want that. My goal is to give you the mindset tools that'll allow you to be the best version of your entrepreneurial self. The one that will kick fear to the curb, release you from the box that everyone else tries to put you in, and have you stepping into the leader role you're meant to have.

In order to do that, we've got to first address those fears. They're the things nagging at you and holding you back from what you want to achieve. These include all the things that you tell yourself in your mind repeatedly about whether you really know what you're doing, whether you should put yourself out there, or even whether you're better off staying in your comfort zone. That's because it's completely in our nature to be comfortable and to have thoughts that keep us in that safe space. Why rock the boat when you're fine where you are? But what if rocking that boat actually meant getting out of the giant ocean you've been going around in circles in and moving onto a beautiful island that has absolutely everything you could ever need or want? If you knew you could get to that island and finally be where you want to be, wouldn't you rock that boat?

It's so much easier said than done, especially when you're in a place where you feel stuck and frustrated that you're never gonna get to where you want to be. I'm gonna be blunt here though, and tell you that no matter how uncomfortable you are with the idea of change, right now change is the thing you need the most. It's where you're going to learn the biggest lessons and accomplish the greatest things that not only feed your soul but make the impact you want to make on the world. If you choose to stay comfortable instead of addressing your fears, then the lessons you're meant to learn now will just show up in another shape or form somewhere down the road. So it's best to just confront what's in your way now and get on with the path toward fulfilling your purpose by using your gifts.

First of all, fear is a very powerful thing and can be seriously stifling. There are so many different blocks that can come up as an entrepreneur, but you need to ask yourself one fundamental question: which is more powerful for you, the fear of stepping up and taking action toward your dream or the regret of not having tried at all? When you're eighty years old, what is it that you want to remember about your life? That you didn't at least try to achieve what you wanted or that you shared your gifts? Think about how that would feel to you on your deathbed if you had to consider the possibility of all the things you could have done but didn't. That's a devastating thought for someone about to no longer be here.

Do you really want to spend years nagging at yourself over the things holding you back only to finally in the end have nothing to show for your time here? It may be a considerable challenge right now to even get started and find the way to achieve the life and business you want, but you will feel so much better knowing that you tried at the very least. Even in failure there's always some relief in knowing that you put in the effort and you learned some kind of lesson out of it all. Even if things don't go the way you hope they do, you can always grow from it. Knowing that, it should lighten the weight you feel a bit by understanding that you ultimately can't fail. You can only grow.

Now that's all well and good, but what about all those fears and blocks still standing in your way and keeping you from making any real progress? To get you passed staying stagnant in those fears, you've got to ask yourself, "What's the worst that could happen?" Play devil's advocate with your mind because it's continually telling you things that have you living in this state of fear. So you have to turn whatever it is that's bothering you on it's head and be the opposition, just as you would if you were a politician running against an opponent. Think about the fears that are coming up for you and what your counter-arguments would be just as if you were battling an opponent in a debate. Only this time, instead of being the negative one telling yourself that you can't do something, you're the one advocating for change and improvement. You're the one standing in the face of the challenge and rising to the occasion. You're the one dismissing the fear with strong arguments for why that fear is made up, lacks substance, and has no real basis in reality.

Action Exercise:

Use this exercise to unlock the fears that may be holding you back and start to bring them to light. By doing this, you allow yourself to confront what's keeping you stagnant and begin to find ways to look at things differently to progress. Give yourself some quiet time to sit with your thoughts for this exercise and really devote your attention to where your blocks may be coming from at their core.

Start by going through the scenario in your head about what you think could potentially happen if you put yourself out there and did what you wanted to do. What would that mean for you? Do you think you'd be out of time, money, or something more substantial like your health? Or is it how you might feel or what people might say about you that's got you worried?

Come up with a list of all the things swirling around in your head that are making you afraid to build a business that you actually want. Get them all out and then review what it would be like if they actually happened. If you're being honest with yourself, do any of those things really matter to you in the long run or are they more important than achieving the success you know you can achieve? If any of those things did happen, where people made fun of you or you lost money or anything else, what could you do to move past those things and turn them around for the better?

What you're really asking yourself here is if what you're afraid of actually did happen, so what? It may be that you just have to pivot and go a different route. It may be that you have to pay a price in one area of your life to achieve a version of success that actually makes you fulfilled. It may mean that the path to get to where you want to go gets a lot longer. But really, so what? If the path you're on is a moral one that follows your true compass and doesn't hurt others along the way, then why worry about the rest? There will be setbacks and forks in the road, but it'll be up to you to decide how to approach them. You are fully capable of steering the situation to keep you on track, no matter what comes your way in the process. Plus, with the help of some gut checks and your own intuition, you can weather any storm that may come.

But understand this: there comes a point where you have to let go of the things that are burdening you and trust that the universe will guide you to where you need to go. Once you understand that, things become a whole lot easier to reconcile along the way. You can begin to let go of some of that control and the tight grip that you've had over staying in your comfort zone in order to realize that everything will be okay. You are meant to be your best self. If you can move past the fear into a place where you're willing to be guided and able to assume the role you're meant to play in your own success, then your path will unfold before you. That's when you'll be able to see your vision coming to fruition.

———————————

There are some very specific blocks that most people go through along their path. If you can confront these head on and recognize if they're coming up for you again, you'll be able to direct your energy to not only dispelling them quickly but also to sail right passed them on your way to the next mile marker on your journey. Thus, in this section, I'm going to cover the biggest blocks and fears that you're likely to face or are facing right now. I'll show you how to identify them and put yourself in the right frame of mind to ditch those fears as quickly as possible. Let's get right to it.

The first block you may be experiencing is you're engaged in too much planning and not enough action. This is one that gets me over and over again (if I'm being honest) because it's in my nature to be a planner. That's really where my comfort zone lies, and I'll quite frequently have to catch myself in a constant cycle of planning and not enough action when it's not serving me well. This is one that I know plagues many other multi-passionate people as well. It's so easy to keep spinning in different directions while you're putting all of the pieces together in your head for how to achieve your goals. Yet, you're not going in any clear direction. Your planning is keeping you scattered when the intent of it is actually the opposite. See, there comes a point where more planning is actually preventing you from moving forward, no matter how much it may seem otherwise. If this is true for you, then you can see it by looking at the real results you're getting for your efforts.

Let's look at the field of city planning as an example to understand this a little bit further. For each locality, there is a document called the master plan. It usually consists of a plan detailing out the specific design and economic intentions of the area for a set number of years into the future. Usually, it's a five or ten-year plan. Everything is organized, regarding what the town hopes to see as far as growth and development in the coming years and the standards they plan to uphold. Now, this document is the baseline for their intentions, but it is not the actionable projects that will get the town to where it needs to be. It doesn't include any implementation of real estate development, any business contracts, or any community actions. It's just a guide, and a very well thought out and detailed guide at that. However, that's where it stops short of getting any real results.

Without implementing actual building projects or starting conversations to get larger businesses to move to the area or other engaging community activities, it all just looks good on paper. The results are in the doing. I admit, there have been many nights where I've found myself creating and recreating my own ten-year master plan, only to have my husband roll his eyes at me again. That's when I know that I'm stuck in my over-planning loop, and I have to do a double-take to see if that planning is actually serving me well to get results. A lot of the time, I've been in my head so badly that I just keep going over my plans again and again, trying to make them perfect before actually implementing any of it. I do this for not only my business but for our family life as well.

This is probably the biggest thing that has kept me stuck for so long, and something that is deeply rooted in my inherent nature. When you're dealing with being an over-planner, sometimes it feels like you're fighting yourself to get past it because you're so compelled to be prepared that you don't know any other way to do things. You can't even fathom leaping without first knowing exactly what path lies in front of you. The thing is, though, that anything done in excess is usually going to be to your detriment, and that's really the case here as well. As an entrepreneur without the safety net of a guaranteed-to-work plan, you've got to see what works in reality to be successful. It may be scary to let go of the reins and jump in. I know it's scary for me with any new venture to put myself out there and do something different. However, getting out of your own head and testing your ideas and work out in the real world is the best way to move forward.

There could be any number of reasons why you may still be in perpetual planning mode. Maybe you're still trying to find that one right calling that's just for you, or maybe you're trying to figure out how to incorporate several passions into one business. No matter what you feel like you need to plan more thoroughly, the bottom line is that it's not helping you make forward progress. The only way to do that is to put down your planner and take action in some way, shape, or form. Any action that gets you moving and implementing will help to gradually squash the need to consistently over-plan.

On top of that, if you allow faith in yourself to become your new best friend on this journey, you'll start to see results even quicker than if you were planning with a lack of faith. This allows you to move forward through positivity and question yourself much less than if you didn't believe what you wanted was possible. Not only does believing in yourself move you forward, but it also attracts others. Confidence is contagious. It helps others to see you in a new light as a strong individual who knows his or her value and capabilities. Others will feel the confidence and faith you have in yourself and want to engage with you more. So by exuding confidence, you can give yourself that little nudge you need to move out of planning mode and have the faith that you can do this.

Whatever you're planning right now, just know that you are not the only one who feels like things need to be planned perfectly before you actually do them. It's a block, yes, but not an impasse. If you are a habitual planner like I am, then take heart that it does get easier the more action you take. While a solid plan is an amazing tool to have in your entrepreneurial toolbox, action ultimately will get you to where you want to go. No matter what the result of that action, you can turn it into growing confidence in yourself as you learn. So nip this block right in the bud as soon as you can, and take action immediately, no matter how big or small that action may be. I bet you'll gain momentum after that first step and move onto the next one quickly thereafter.

––––––––––––––––

Alright, now that you have a notion of whether this particular block may be affecting you, I want to break it up into two different parts so you can clearly identify what it is about planning that's causing your stagnation. First of all, there's analysis paralysis. This one is where you continually analyze things over and over to see if you can make sense of it. It may be about what you're doing, whether it's right for your audience, if it sounds good, or if it will sell. In your head, you may be thinking that you're taking action because you're planning things out, making carefully calculated decisions, and tailoring your adjustments to what you find. However, even though what you're doing is making changes on paper, no real progress is being made to increase the growth of your business since there's no real action involved. You just keep analyzing things and doing more research to try to work things out in your head rather than by doing them to gain clarity or verification in real life application.

Overanalyzing can greatly play into your fears and cause you to stagnate. Psychologist Barry Schwartz discusses how an enormous amount of choices and unlimited access to information ultimately leads to indecision and paralysis.[12] Instead of enabling us, it actually keeps us from moving forward because we're stuck with too many choices.[13] Another team consisting of psychologists Sian Beilock and Thomas Carr, describe short-term working memory as the sweet spot for accomplishing tasks.[14] They maintain that what allows us

---

[12] https://www.ted.com/talks/
barry_schwartz_on_the_paradox_of_choice?
language=en#t-470586

[13] https://www.ted.com/talks/
barry_schwartz_on_the_paradox_of_choice?
language=en#t-470586

[14] https://blog.todoist.com/2015/07/08/analysis-paralysis-and-your-productivity/

to focus and get things done is that limited amount of relevant information that we receive without distractions. "If the ability of working memory to maintain task focus is disrupted, performance may suffer."[15] Studies have shown that both distractions as well as anxiety cause productivity to decrease. Overanalyzing on top of feeling anxious only draws you further away from productivity.[16]

Let me be blunt for you here in case you need a strong dose of tough love: the needle moves from action and trying things in real life, not by doing them in your head or on paper. It took me years to take action on my plans and to even decide what to offer in the first place. Before that I was going in circles with a million ideas, changing them every five seconds based on what I thought people would like, and then changing them again as I changed my business vision. While there is validity in testing things out with a target market, in my case, I was in a never-ending cycle of doing busy work on my own that didn't really amount to tangible results. Of course, from the outside looking in, I was always working hard on my offerings, and to me, I thought I was doing things the right way as I was trying to be methodical and calculated. Turns out, I was spinning my wheels when all I

[15] https://blog.todoist.com/2015/07/08/analysis-paralysis-and-your-productivity/

[16] https://blog.todoist.com/2015/07/08/analysis-paralysis-and-your-productivity/

really needed was to get out there and work with people.

Analyzing and researching your business ideas, your audience, or anything else is necessary up to a certain point. Once you understand the basics of those things and have a solid footing to start, then you just need to get out there and launch it. You've got to come to terms with the fact that there's only so much research you can do sitting in your office. You need to talk with potential customers, coach real people needing your help, and actually ask people what they're interested in buying to solve their problems. Then, you bite the bullet and put something out there. I know, it's scary to jump in, but it's a requirement for progress if you want to run your own business.

Moving beyond planning procrastination and into doing the hard tasks is necessary for growth. Analyzing something to death won't give you that final version that you're looking for anyway, so come to terms with putting out a minimum viable offer (one that's the quickest and easiest to test out at first) that will allow you to see what resonates with people and what doesn't. You can pretty much guarantee that the response you'll get will be different in some way from what you were thinking in your head just by researching. You just never would have realized that difference if you only paid attention to your thoughts instead of what worked for others.

Now that you've got the first piece of over-planning dealt with, what about the second? The second one is quite frankly an epidemic. It's being in perfection mode. In perfection mode, you're stuck making everything perfect before you can even get it out the door. So you work hard on a project or an offer, continue to refine it, and tweak it over and over again without launching it because you're afraid that it just won't be quite right. This perfectionism can be about anything from writing a book to publishing your website or even launching a course. It's one of those things that'll most likely plaque you for a long time into the future as well, so you must try to nip it in the bud early and find ways to continually override that perfectionist feeling when it creeps in again.

To start getting over it, ask yourself again, what's the worst that would happen if you published or launched your work the way that it currently is? Would it be the end of the world or would you actually be able to learn something from it? In all likelihood, you're going to be able to learn something no matter what, so it's always best to err on the side of doing rather than waiting. You need to think about it from that angle yourself, though, and truly decide what could be so bad about launching your work the way that it is. Then, think about the opposite of that question. What if you never launched or published your work because it never felt completely right to you? How would you feel about that? If that's not an option for you or you don't want it to be, then you have your answer right there.

When you're feeling afraid of putting your work out there until it's exactly right, what's really happening is that your ego is getting in your way and taking over your thinking. You're putting way too much emphasis on you and what it means for you if you put work out that isn't quite right...how you might be judged, what people might think of you, or even why anyone would buy it. That's really all about you, and we want to change that mentality to be about those you're serving. How could you not publish or launch when people are waiting for it to help them? How can you keep this work to yourself when it could affect someone's life for the better? No matter how imperfect the thing you're working on may be, it'll still be helpful in some capacity to someone out there. That's all it needs to be.

I've learned from doing countless projects over the years that things will never be fully complete or even to a place of my complete liking. There will always be something that I still want to adjust and make better. That's just the nature of things. Give yourself that deadline and tell yourself that you can't make it perfect by keeping it to yourself. It'll never happen. However, what you can do is send it out into the world to get feedback so that you can make adjustments that really support the people who need it most. That's the real power of action over stagnation. You will be able to move closer to a better product once you get people's opinions and reviews. It just doesn't happen unless you put it out there, and it certainly won't ever be fully perfect.

It can be scary to potentially hear that people may not like your work or appreciate it, especially when you've put so much of yourself into it. This is something I struggled with and learned throughout getting my bachelor's degree in architecture. We had peer reviews of our designs at least once a month in our studio classes and public reviews of our work at least twice a semester. It was brutal at times. People would painstakingly work on their building models for months and stayed up for several nights straight to complete them, only to have them be torn apart physically and verbally by a professor who found several flaws in the design.

It was an incredibly crushing experience to a lot of people and was definitely not a program for the faint of heart or for those who did not have broad shoulders. I specifically remember a time during my own public design review where I had been up for two nights straight, running on no sleep, had been working myself into the ground, and I knew that what I was presenting was not my best work. I was low on energy and creative inspiration, and I just didn't have much to give then. So during my design review, the professors on the review board had a field day with my design. Although they did not physically tear up my model, they did verbally tear into the feasibility of the design. I knew everyone could tell I was upset, and I was doing everything I could to hold back the tears in my eyes. I kept it together as best I could, though, said thank you to the reviewers for their comments, and went straight to the bathroom to cry my eyes out.

At that moment, I didn't have it in me to fight or even defend my design. I was exhausted, and I knew on some level they were right. I also knew, though, that I put myself out there. I had the guts to at least put something together, present it publicly, and get trashed in the process. No matter how much that stung, it also helped me toughen up to the idea that putting my work out into the world was a requirement for making progress. I needed the feedback, the judgment, and the harsh criticism to make it better. The tears and the upset were a result of me putting myself into my work so intensely and pouring myself into what I did. However, when it came down to it and I sent my work out into the world, it no longer should have been about me. It should have been about what the project needed to be and what the user of that building needed and wanted. That's why the critics were so harsh. That's why they tore it apart. It had nothing to do with how I felt or how I poured countless hours into it. It had everything to do with collaborating to ensure the project was the best it could possibly be for the end client.

We get so close to the work that we do that a lot of the time it becomes personal. That can be where the perfectionism starts to creep in and make us afraid to put it out there until it's just right. Sometimes you subconsciously equate that work or project to yourself and the judgment people may have for the work then gets jumbled up with you as the creator. You've got to loosen your grip a bit and find a way to detach yourself from your process. You may pour every ounce of yourself into what you're doing, but it is not a direct reflection of you. It's an expression of the inspiration that came through you and your gifts, and it can only be made better by more discussion and reviews outside of yourself.

What you're planning may seem great to you on paper. Yet, when you present it to someone, it may turn out to be confusing or miss the mark to what they actually need. That just means that adjustments are needed. It's probably not that you need to scrap the whole thing because it's a big failure. If you can find ways to separate your feelings from the judgment of the work, then you can look beyond any negative comments or reviews and use them to make your work better. That's the whole point. Perfectionism doesn't exist, but collaborative improvements do. Use your imperfect work as a starting point for a discussion with your audience. When people are excited about an idea or concept that could help them, they're more than willing to be part of the process to make it better.

By taking yourself out of the equation, you're opening yourself up to comments and improvement. That's a huge shift from working in a vacuum all by yourself and trying to make things perfect. Instead, you can invite people to share in the project and encourage them to help make it even better. Think about the possibilities once that happens. You can seriously reduce the stress on yourself over making your work perfect, and you can start building honest relationships with people in the process. So rather than dreading the idea of putting out something imperfect, build it into the conversation with your tribe and ask for constructive criticism or suggestions moving forward. Then the next time you launch, it'll be that much closer to what the market truly wants and needs.

Now that I've made that point, let me backup a step and talk to you about your initial offer, or minimum viable product. In creating it, it's especially important to detach yourself from the work and allow it to be imperfect. You'll want to launch as soon it as possible to get feedback. You'll be able to see people's responses to it and how your work actually affects them. This first thing you do is most likely not going to be the last thing you do by any stretch. So realize that you're going to get some harsh criticism. That's okay because this is just the beginning of a learning experience. It's a test, not the end all be all.

Set yourself up with your initial work being an experiment and every new thing you do as an experiment as well. It'll relieve so much pressure to be perfect, and you can tell yourself in your mind that any critiques will serve to enhance future versions of it. The things that actually do work will be the ones that will most likely become your core offers. Remember, you have the ability to shape your offers uniquely to create a very tailored experience for your customers, so feedback is important to find out what works. Then, for your next launch, you'll be off to the races!

One last note I'd like to make about over-planning, though, is that this particular block may not be one that goes softly into the night. What I mean by that is that it'll come back again and again, especially if you're a planning-focused person. I want to encourage you to not abandon your plans altogether because they are essential in order to know where you're headed. Instead, keep this mindset about serving others and delivering what they need first and foremost. By taking yourself out of it and releasing the feeling of being judged, you'll have a surefire way to kick this block to the curb in the future.

Another block that may be tripping you up is what I consider to be consuming rather than giving. This one puts you in a headspace where you think you need to be more of an expert than you are or have more knowledge than you do currently. You may continually buy courses and programs or try to get more certifications or experience, but you never quite feel like you're accomplished or experienced enough to get out there and get started. It can be so easy to fall into this trap these days. There are so many marketers out there with amazing webinars to pitch you the latest and greatest strategies or coaches that guarantee they'll help you succeed. So you end up getting this "shiny object syndrome," going from one strategy or training to the next and always feeling like you need something more than you actually do.

The core of shiny object syndrome has a lot to do with judging yourself and feeling like it's all about you even though you don't realize it. You may feel like you're inadequate in some way when you look at others in your same industry. They may have more credentials, more followers, a better resume, or better business numbers. That could be making you feel like you need to do more or be more than you are. You may feel like an imposter who's just playing around in your chosen field where others have a greater background in the subject than you do. You may even feel like you need to learn all the strategies of how to grow your business before you even start so that you can begin on the right foot.

First of all, if this is the case for you, you're still stuck in the mindset of needing to be a single-focused specialist in your career. This happens when already knowledge-able or experienced multi-passionate people feel like imposters or like they need to know more before helping others. Letting go of the idea that you need to have all the knowledge on a subject in order to teach it or sell things related to it will allow you to see how many people you actually can help at the current moment. You always have something to offer to help someone else, no matter what level you're at yourself.

There will always be room to grow and improve, and you can do that throughout your journey. At the present moment, though, you're exactly where you need to be in order to help someone who's not at your level yet. I guarantee you have a large amount of expertise in several areas as a multi-passionate entrepreneur, and you've got that unique positioning to give you a tailored approach to solving problems. Just because you haven't taken every course out there or you don't have a specific certification doesn't mean you can't still be of service. Start where you are. Give people the chance to see the value you already have to help them exactly where they are now, too.

Action Exercise:

I want you to think about how much you know about each subject you're passionate about and what you can teach people right now. Make a list in each area of expertise about specific things you know and can teach. Write the subject areas at the top of your paper and below each one identify the specific items. Jot down everything you can think of no matter how small or large. It could be as small as helping someone choose an appropriate outfit for a party or as large as how to grow a profitable business.

Nothing is out of the question when you're making this list of knowledge and expertise. Think of it as what you could teach if you were just teaching them for an hour, a day, a week, or an entire semester. This will give you a baseline for ideas ranging from small to large. Once you're done, review your list and look at all of the possibilities. If you only wrote down a few items, then go back through the exercise again. This time, take at least five minutes for each subject and break them down into what each subject entails. Then, jot down your knowledge about those detailed pieces. After doing that, go back through each subject and write down something broad that you could teach about each one.

Review your list another time to gain some perspective on how much you have to draw from already. Anything you wrote down can be uniquely applied to creating an offering or even a business around it, and you can tailor each item to your perspective. Thus, just from this list alone, you can see that you already have the knowledge you need to help someone and to make an impact. Going forward, refer back to this list to show you just how capable you are at the current moment and how unnecessary it is to look outside yourself for the answers anymore.

There are definitely plenty of people out there who need specific expertise, even if it may just be a small thing. As a small example of what I need in my own life, I know I for one would love help with how to get yeast to actually work and get bread to rise! Cooking and baking is something I love to do, but for some reason I just can never get bread to rise! If someone solved that problem for me, I would be pretty happy. On the other hand, I've got bigger issues to solve as well! As a parent, there are some things that I would just love someone else to solve for me. For example, we've had lots of issues with getting my oldest to sleep well. It's been such an issue for us that we've sought out sleep coaches and professionals in the area of children's sleep so that we could find realistic solutions to the problems our family struggles with regularly.

No experience level is too small to help someone unless it's zero. In your case, you've taken the time to dive into your interest areas, learn about subjects you're interested in, and get knowledgeable about things that fuel your soul. So feeling like you don't have what it takes yet to help someone and that you just need a bit more training or knowledge is really just all in your head. Yes, knowledge is always desirable, and in all probability you are a lifelong learner. That is something to be commended. However, it's time to realize that you are already enough with what you have in your knowledge arsenal.

Moving to the second point regarding consuming rather than giving, you're letting your ego get in your way just as in the perfectionism block. When you say your work isn't good enough yet, that places way too much attention on judging yourself. It's time to shift your mindset to the people who need your work in their lives rather than you as the creator. They need the help you can give them at this moment in time. No matter what credentials you currently have or what state your work is currently in, there is value in it. All you have to do is engage with your community openly and honestly about what you have to offer them now and how that can provide what they need.

Let's think for a second about how this would go over with someone if they came across you online with your current amount of expertise. Would they be saying, "Wow, she really has all the information I need and the approach that makes sense to me. If only she had two letters after her name for a certification, then maybe I could actually work with her?" In all likelihood, that's not going to be the case. I mean, do you ask every person you do business with where they went to school, for how many years, and exactly who they've worked with? Of course, not! You trust in most cases that a professional saying they can deliver results will actually be able to get you those results. Most of the time, they have testimonials and reviews that you go to the most for verification.

The point is, though, that your ideal audience is out there right now looking for someone with the solution that you have. Once they see that you've got it, that's all that will matter. They're only concerned with how desperately they need your help, and that you can actually deliver results for them. You're the only person who may be obsessing over how you got the knowledge you have or why you need even more. You may be self-taught, learned by accident, took a couple of online courses, coached a handful of people, or even got a degree. Any of those things are valid enough for you to teach what you know to someone else without feeling like you're not good enough.

The way you need to approach this block is by telling yourself that you are already enough. You can always help someone that knows less about a subject than you do. If you've got a way of thinking or approaching a problem that just makes sense for them and makes it click like no one else can, then they're going to work with you over anyone else. Helping them get to their end goal is all that matters, and I guarantee you're already all that you need to be in this current moment to help someone. There are a few of questions to ask yourself when you're trying to reframe your mindset here. How would the people who need your work feel if they never found you? Would anyone be able to help them in the same way that you can? What would happen if your message and work didn't get out into the world?

These are the extremely valuable questions to contemplate when you really need to see the value in what you have to offer, no matter what stage of the game you're at. Your mindset shift around the value you provide is a critical turning point not only at this beginning stage to get you out there into the marketplace but also to confirm along the way that you are capable of being successful. That means that you shouldn't be afraid of charging your worth and working with customers who also value your work highly in their lives. So every time you catch yourself thinking that you need more experience or to learn something else before putting your work out there, tell yourself that you shouldn't be making your community wait for what they need. Take yourself out of the equation and put the focus on them. Then, you can decide whether more knowledge would actually help you improve your results or whether you're just letting judgment get in your way.

Getting onto the next block, I'm going to be quite vulnerable here with you on this one. I've fought the idea that my circumstances were holding me back for as long as I can remember, and you may be unintentionally doing this as well. In my own life, being a military spouse has been the biggest hurdle of all in this department. If you're unfamiliar with what it means to be a military family, then it may be hard to understand how constraining it feels at times. I'll walk you through a bit of it from my perspective and how it really took a toll on my entrepreneurial mindset for so long.

Now, I've been an active duty officer, a civil servant, and now a veteran and ready reservist. All of that time, I've also been a military spouse. I have to say, though, that when it comes to establishing and furthering my career, I never realized how much being a military spouse was going to have a major effect on me until that was my day-to-day lifestyle. As we moved from place to place, sometimes in the span of only months, having to pick up our lives and start fresh in each spot including overseas, the idea of having my own career and business seemed incredibly challenging, sometimes even defeating.

I had been a military officer with an architecture degree. I had overseen multi-million dollar design and construction projects. I had planned and led teams to implement major events. Plus, I had also gone back to school to advance my training and get my masters degree. Yet, the further away from leaving my standard day job and the further into being an at-home military spouse I got, the more I felt a total lack of control when it came to my career. There were so many times where I felt like I was never going to be able to have a career of my own again. Where I was being dragged around and the military was taking priority over every ounce of our lives. While it is safe to say that a military family does give up a lot of control over their lives and makes incredible sacrifices every single day, I do have to be honest with myself and recognize that the way I was looking at the situation was only making it worse.

As we lived overseas in England and Japan for about eight years (something I had wanted to do for my entire life), all I could really focus on during that time was what an obstacle it was in starting my business, networking, and launching anything meaningful. I felt like I never had a big enough pool of people for my business to grow because we were always tied to a small military community. I didn't feel like I could really market locally being under certain visa requirements or not even speaking the language. I resigned myself to testing out different business ideas online mostly but always had an underlying mindset that my circumstances were standing in my way. It wasn't until we moved back to the states and had our second child that I realized how much time I had wasted worrying about my circumstances and how impossible they seemed to make everything. Leave it to having kids to make you remember how good you had it when you were on your own with all the time in the world! It finally started clicking, though, at that point that I was the one standing in my own way, not anything else.

Everything under the sun can be a projection if you let it so that eventually you just feel like everything is stacked up against you. That doesn't have to be the way you look at things, though. You don't have to let your circumstances dictate your reality. You should actually be building a positive mindset around what's currently in your life and thus creating the circumstances of your choosing. You have the choice to be grateful for what is good in your life and figure out how to make the most of what you have to work with currently. You've got the ability to think about your situation differently and decide that you're going to make any changes you possibly can to alter your own reality. There's always a choice, and blaming your circumstances serves no one, least of all you.

I stood in my way for so long and decided that I could only do things one way and that way wasn't going to work with my current situation. So I wasn't flexible or adaptable in my mindset or my actions. I wasn't reframing the way I was looking at my career and how I could put myself back in control as an entrepreneur. It doesn't have to be that way for you. By waking up to your own capability to see the positive and then finding ways to adapt, you can still stay on track toward the vision you hope to create for your life and business. All it really takes is to realize that if there's a will, there's always a way.

Possibly, the way I thought I was supposed to build a business wasn't going to be right for me anyway. Maybe the universe was helping me to see that I needed to be more flexible or even to put others needs above my own at that point. As I started to make these realizations and see beyond a set of constraints, I was able to start undoing the thinking that was keeping me boxed in and stuck for so long. Now, I'm not one to have regrets. In all honesty, though, if I had only opened myself up to seeing other possibilities and realizing that I was creating my own reality, I would have been a lot less anxious. I would have been able to give myself some grace for getting to where I wanted to be. Hindsight is twenty-twenty.

That's why I'm sharing this story with you to help you understand that your circumstances are not what's holding you back. It's your mindset. You have the power to achieve the success you want no matter what your circumstances may be because you can always look at things differently, create a different approach to what you want, be more flexible with a solution, or just more gracious in what you do have going for you. It's quite frankly all in your head, and the sooner you realize that, the better off you'll be in all that you do.

As an interjection, when I talk about being mindful of changing your circumstances, I'm assuming that you are an adult, or close to it, in a circumstance that is not life-threatening or harmful to an extreme. I'm assuming that you most likely have established a certain mindset around what's going on in your life to the point that it's been holding you back, while in actuality you do have the ability to make that shift to change things. Granted, everyone's circumstances are different in what we live with every single day, and some quite frankly have severe hardships. For you, though, I'm going out on a limb to say that you most likely have the ability to change your mindset and improve your life.

To actually do this, we need to go back to the saying, "where there's a will, there's a way." The way things have been going for you may not be working, so you need to put forth a bit of energy to get the ball moving in the right direction. Nothing will shift unless you exert that energy to alter the current state of things. Just as in physics, every action has a reaction. If you start by giving your business a nudge forward in a way that you haven't done before and create a force to get the ball moving in a different way, then there will be a reaction. It's inherent in nature. All things flow from energy, and this is a great initial step to acknowledge that you do in fact have the power to create change.

Next, look at the things you have been doing to grow your business. What are the excuses you've been making for why things aren't progressing for you? How have you approached those specific areas? If it's just by shrugging and thinking you can't do anything about it or being resigned to what's happening to you instead of you being in control, then it's time to think differently about it. What are three ways that you could look at your situation as a positive thing? What can be learned or strengthened because of it? There's always a lesson or a take-away even in the worst of situations.

Having gratitude for what you can receive in your situation is the second part of altering your reality. How can you see what's in your way as a meaningful experience rather than an obstacle? Find some iota of gratefulness that you can latch onto and start to see things in a positive light. This will take away some of the bitterness and negativity that you may be feeling for not being able to make progress. It's always important to open yourself up to where you currently are so that the energy you actually express won't be in vain. Otherwise, you'll still be operating from a point of exhaustion and discontentment. Turning this around, however, and combining both positivity and momentum in a new direction can result in some great progress.

Let me give you an example. Let's say that you want to start a wedding photography business since you're passionate about people finding someone to share their lives with. You're in a lot of debt, though. You can't afford to buy the equipment you feel you need to get ahead in your business. It would take flashes, backdrops, new lenses, and new computer software to be able to do large scale weddings. So you've resigned yourself to never being able to realize this dream as you've got mounds of debt in your way. What if you shifted your perspective and looked at it from a place of gratitude instead? If you made just a couple simple changes, it could mean a world of difference.

Instead of holding onto those feelings of being stuck, you could decide to first change your thinking and create a little energy and forward momentum for yourself. You may decide to ask around to some friends who are getting married soon to see if they'd be interested in doing a mini engagement photo session with you for only one hundred dollars. You could tell them that you don't have the equipment for their entire wedding, but you'd love to help them out beforehand as they celebrate the days leading up to the big event. In doing so, you've just created a force moving your business in a different direction than you had previously.

Next, you decide to be more positive about your situation. You could look at the equipment you do have and realize that you can easily do a bunch of engagement sessions for couples without needing all the equipment you would for an entire wedding. You start to become grateful that you have the skill set and talent to take beautiful photos that people will love. You let go of the worry of having to do big weddings because doing these engagement photos feels fulfilling. You make a list of all the people you know who are in the season of their lives where they're starting meaningful relationships. That solidifies the idea that you have a network of friends and community members who know and like you already and who would love it if you could support them with the special moments in their lives. So the gratefulness builds, and you start to see how that can, in turn, allow you to pay off your debt over time. It starts with small actions, being grateful for what is going well, and building up to the bigger picture of what you want.

Many times we're in our own heads about our own lives, much to our detriment. Once you see that and allow yourself to take purposeful action alongside being thankful for what is working, your eyes will open. Your reality will start to shift because you're making a change. Now, you have to have the will for this. You must determine in your own mind that you have the power to make that change and that you're ready for it to happen. It must be something you know in your gut so that you don't waiver with your capability to create results in your life.

_____

Action Exercise:

To jumpstart change in your life, you need to assess what's really going on right now and what changes you'd like to make. Set aside some time for a brainstorming session in a quiet place where you can organize your thoughts. Write down what it is that has been bothering you or feeling like a roadblock in your life. Be specific if you can and include the emotions you feel in your current situation. Then, think about what specific change you want to make. Write down how you would like to feel and what needs to change to get you there.

List all of the ways that you could improve your situation right now. How can you get from what you're currently feeling to what you want to be feeling? Can you use any resources you may have or people you know? Could you use another skill that you've learned? Can you deliver your offer differently or present it differently? How could you use where you're located to your advantage? Think about pivoting from the way you've been doing things and brainstorm in a totally different direction. No idea is too small or not worth it here. Expand out of what you'd normally think is feasible, and let your mind go to any ideas you may have.

Look at the list of brainstorming ideas that you've made, and put a number next to each one from one to five according to how easy they would be to implement, with one being the easiest. Next, go down your list and put a star next to each idea that would have the most impact on moving you in the right direction for your business. Are there any ideas that have both a star and a low number? If so, those are the easiest to implement for you right now, and they'll have the highest return. Therefore, those are the ones you need to look at doing right away and focus your attention on doing. If you can implement even one or two of those things, that may just be enough for you to see a small shift in your circumstances and your reality, so much so that it's possible to take that momentum and drive you forward even more in the direction you're hoping to be headed.

Now, in addition to your list of changes to implement, you also want to make a gratitude list. On a separate sheet of paper, write down all of the things that are going well for you or that you have to be thankful for in your life. No matter how bad things seem now, there is always something to be thankful for in your life. It can be anything from being able to buy groceries all the way to having a supportive spouse. Getting it all out on paper right down to the littlest things can serve as a great reminder to you that it's all about perspective.

Each night before bed, our family does what we call our "thankful time." We share what we are grateful for that day. Sometimes it's that we got to eat pizza for dinner. Sometimes it's that we had a family vacation. Regardless of what we're each thankful for, the important part is that we take the time to acknowledge what is beautiful in our lives.

Your gratitude list is just as important for you here. Use it to confirm to yourself that there is always something working in your favor. If you can keep the items on your list in mind and reference them as you take steps to make change, then you'll relieve some of the weight on your shoulders. It can help you feel lighter knowing that things are on your side, and it's all a matter of perspective.

_____

The final block that I want to talk about could be underlying and something that you've never even realized. However, strange as it may seem, you could be sabotaging your own success if you're afraid of what comes with that success. There can be a number of things that you've associated with being successful subconsciously. It could be due to some connection you've made to those things or an experience you've had. It's possible that you've been steering yourself clear of success as a precautionary measure. Sounds ridiculous, right? Actually, when you think through it, the things that come with success can actually seem scary at first.

You may be thinking about devoting your time to one business for an entire decade, the possibility of being in charge of several employees, generating millions of dollars in revenue, or having to speak in front of a crowd of hundreds. Those can all be really daunting, especially if you're not at all used to that. It's okay to be afraid of things that are unfamiliar to you and that you may have experienced as bad previously. Change is not something that people generally take to easily. You may need to ease your way into it if you find that taking the plunge and diving right in just isn't a good fit for you personally. Just know that the changes that come from getting out of your comfort zone into a place with potentially higher stakes and greater responsibility are all par for the course in this entrepreneurship journey. So at some point, if you want to carve your own path badly enough, you're going to have to battle this fear head-on.

If bringing this up strikes a chord with you, then there may be something in your background, the way you were brought up, or even the way business has been presented to you that's making you afraid of your own success. If you can recognize it, then you can find ways to move past it. The tricky part is identifying it, and the best way to do that is to be totally honest with yourself about what makes you nervous, scared, or downright terrified. It takes some real introspection to figure this out, but once you do, you can make some decisions about where you're headed. This is especially important as a multi-passionate entrepreneur because your version of success most likely won't look like the traditional idea of it. You probably are going to have to do more soul-searching to get to the heart of what's making you cringe compared to the things that you actually do want. If your block is rooted in the way standard businesses look and feel, then that's easily fixed with some strategizing. You won't know what it is, though, until you take a deeper look.

Let me say, though, that fear of where you're headed could also be a good thing. When you have a big enough vision for what you want, it most likely will scare you a bit in a good way. Think about it. You've never done anything as big as what you hope for in your future. Of course, you're going to feel apprehensive about doing it. It's new, different, and probably requires you to get uncomfortable to make it happen. The nature of being scared relies upon the fact that we don't know what to expect. Things are uncertain because we haven't experienced those things before. Thus, fear sets in, makes us uncomfortable, and stifles us. In the case of having a big dream that you're scared to achieve, fear is a really good thing that's telling you what you need to face.

The thing about being uncomfortable is that it means change is happening, right? If you continually stayed in your comfort zone, then you wouldn't make any forward progress. You'd just keep doing what you've been doing, staying in the same spot, and just wishing for what you wanted to no end. Uncomfortableness is a side effect of moving in the right direction. Think of it as your body's way of telling you that you're no longer stagnant. You've chosen to make a move, right or wrong, that'll shift what's happening in your life. That's exactly what we're hoping to achieve: movement. Forward progress can't be made without any movement. You can't expect that staying on the same trajectory will get you to a different place. If you want to go to California, but you've been headed in the direction of New York, then you can't expect to still get to California without changing course.

Action Exercise:

Take a moment to determine what that big vision is that you have for your business and life. You may have been feeling scared of success, but in reality you may not even want that version of success. In this exercise, you'll be able to get clear about what you want and visualize exactly what it'll look like when you achieve it. Now, I've thrown in a bit of manifestation work here, but you're welcome to skip over those parts if they don't suit you. This exercise can be as pragmatic or as soul-searching as you'd like to make it.

Sit quietly by yourself for at least ten minutes. Make sure you're in a relaxed state where you're not stressed out or worried about anything. Think to yourself that you want to uncover your big why. You want to see the big picture of the way your business and life feels best to you and how it makes an impact on the world. If you'd like, you can ask for guidance from the universe to allow your inner compass to lead you.

Then, in your mind, tell yourself that you're meant to be happy and fulfilled. You are meant to achieve your dreams, and if you let it, the universe will align to what's best for you and allow what's inside of you to truly shine.

Now, ask yourself this set of questions: What does that all look like for you? What would your life look like if everything aligned so that you could achieve exactly what you wanted? How would your business and per-sonal life look? Where would you work and for what hours of the day? How would you work with your customers and what change would you facilitate or what problem would you solve for them? Who would you network with? What platform and tribe of followers would you have? Would you live in a certain place or have the time to do certain things? How do you want to approach balancing your family and career?

Be as specific as you can about the vision you're creating for yourself. Then, the next step is to decide what feelings and emotions you want to feel in that moment when everything is aligned for you. This is the other component to getting in alignment with your vision. You have to really feel what it would be like as if it's already happened. As you think about the big picture vision that you've put together for yourself, say in your mind that it's going to happen. You don't have to worry about it anymore because you're already on your way to making it a reality. The universe will align to get you there.

Sink into the feeling of relief as you think about not having to stress or overly control any part of your journey. Decide in your mind that your big vision will come to fruition, and all you have to do is take aligned action with your inner compass.

––––––––––––

Once you've solidified your big vision, ask yourself if any part of that vision makes you especially nervous. In all likelihood, there should be at least a couple, but the idea is to get to the heart of why you're scared of those things. Is it the amount of money you want to make? Is it the publicity? Is there anything about your vision that makes you feel uneasy or like you just want to curl up in the fetal position and not even try because it's way too far out there as a concept?

Hone in on that feeling and dig a little deeper into it until you figure out exactly why you feel that way. It could be a past experience with money, family, business, or anything else. You may be subconsciously carrying over past emotions tied to success and just haven't connected the dots until now. The problem is that those underlying feelings are unresolved and may continue to make you conflicted or even afraid until you nip them in the bud. That's why you need to dig deep and see if something is holding you back because you'll never fully move forward until you address it. It'll just keep coming back up until you do.

If you do find yourself in this situation where you're afraid of some component of your success, the best thing to do is to play the "what if" game. What if I do have to get out there in front of the world? What if I am responsible for a team of people? What if I do make a million dollars? Give yourself a chance to practically think through the scenario that's hindering you and walk through what it would look like. Ask yourself if there are certain steps you can take to combat whatever you're afraid of in that situation. For example, if you're afraid of growing to a certain level, maybe you can put a plan together to hire a financial advisor or an accountant when you get to a certain amount of revenue. Perhaps you can find a mentor to guide you through the team-building process if you're worried about hiring and managing employees effectively.

Ultimately, you have to take back the reins from your fears and decide that you can be proactive in your success. Let go of what's worrying you, choose to remove fear, and act upon your dreams without regret. You can do that by thinking through what could potentially happen and possible solutions so you're prepared. Once you do that, you can let go and move on. Easier said than done, yes, but it'll enable you to make forward progress from a place of positivity rather than worry.

When I was a construction project manager, this was something that we'd do quite a bit for renovation projects. There would always be something that would inevitably go wrong. Sometimes there would be mold or asbestos in an old building, we would uncover termite damage when opening up a wall, or concrete wouldn't set the way it was supposed to for the building foundation. It was extremely important that we looked at any issues we thought may come up before we even started the construction. We needed to address the likelihood of them happening along with how they could affect the timing, cost, or scope of our project. Rarely were we ever deterred from doing a project altogether because of those things. We just had to be mindful of the issues and be prepared. So if you're worried about the possibility of something happening when you do become successful, but you're not even close to the point of being there yet, then just consider what you could do to put your mind at ease with a solid plan.

The bottom line on all of these fears and blocks that we've discussed is that your mind plays a lot of tricks on you. It's your job to see through them in order to create the reality that you actually want. You don't need to listen to others with opinions about what you should be doing. You shouldn't worry about having to know more or struggle with past experiences getting in your way. You always have a choice in releasing those blocks and stepping into the person you want to be and the life you want to have. Be diligent about acknowledging your big vision, pushing through what comes your way with positivity and gratitude, and planning for what you can. Then, just let go of the rest.

Part Two

Strategize Your Path

Chapter Four

Shaping Your Core Message

Niching down is such an uncomfortable thing. However, you do need some kind of focus in order to be successful. This is where your core message or unifying theme comes in to make it all come together. The way you approach this, like anything else, will be dependent upon your viewpoint. The thing that ties all of your genius zones together may be a message, a cause, an idea, or a common interest. No matter which one it is for you, it'll help to create clarity in your business objectives and offerings. For the sake of simplicity as we go through this chapter and beyond, I'll be referring to this as your core message. Just know, though, that it can be any of the unifying things that I mentioned in this paragraph.

Once you discover your core message, it'll essentially take the place of establishing a niche. The very important difference between the two, however, will be that your core message will allow you to expand into multiple interest areas and projects all while showing a clear purpose to your ideal audience, making you not look flaky or confused. You'll be able to take a big sigh of relief knowing that you can still be yourself in everything you like to do, but the focus will remain. Granted, you need to get to the point where you can identify how everything connects. It may not seem like the things you do have any common thread right now, but if you dig a bit deeper, I promise that they do. As you're figuring it out, don't approach it as a common thread that will get you to one tiny focus area. Your core message should be broad enough to encompass your variety of interests and seem more like a big, overarching umbrella for it all.

Action Exercise:

To find your core message that's driving everything you do, sit quietly by yourself for at least ten minutes. Grab a pen and paper or your favorite note-taking application. Make a list of all of your passions, interests, and areas of expertise. Beside each one, write a little note about why you like each of them. What is it about them that spoke to you initially when deciding to learn more about them? What drove you to continue doing them? This will give you a starting point as to why you were drawn to each one.

Below that list, start grouping each of those areas into overarching categories. For example, you may start to see some common categories that are broad like creativity, being family-oriented, or health and wellness. At this point, it's a good idea to think broadly and see how many interests you can actually fit into each category that you've come up with. Can you start to see a common thread that may be present in the majority of them? Look at each interest area from different perspectives to see how it makes the most sense.

Approach your thinking in terms of what could be the underlying message of each of your passions, the cause associated with it, the purpose behind it, or the type of creative outlet or platform that it provides. These are solely jumping off points for you to consider, but they by no means should constrain you in finding common ground.

As you go further and further into your categorizing, you should come down to one broad reason behind everything you do. It may take several rounds of categorizing to find it. Once you get to that point, it should feel like everything totally clicks. The reasoning behind why you're doing all of these things should feel like it completely makes sense in that context and that you finally understand what's driving your work.

What do we mean when we talk about genius zones? Essentially, they're the things that you're incredibly talented at doing. They're things that you could easily create an entire career around by themselves alone because your natural strengths make you good at doing them. You may even have people coming to you all the time for help or advice in some of those areas. Those are your zones of genius, and those are the places where you want to spend the majority of your time in order to make the biggest impact.

While it would be a fantastic career to choose one of those alone and spend your time owning your place in the market, that's not going to fill you up as a multi-passionate person. You've been given each of those genius zones in conjunction with each other for a bigger, overarching reason. It's up to you now to figure out how they can be combined in a way that creates innovation with a new approach or a new way of thinking. That is precisely why you need to get to the heart of your core message if you haven't done so already.

Are you starting to see how incredibly valuable it is to do each of the things you do as part of your greater life's work? One of those areas alone would not create the same impact as having all of them combined in a new and transformative way. One discipline or expertise alone wouldn't ignite change if it were focused on the same perspective as usual. It takes a shift that can only come about through outside thinking and influence—the key thing that you possess as a multi-passionate en-trepreneur. It's a gift to have insight and understanding from multiple disciplines and be able to see how they can interconnect to improve people's lives in some way. That is the point where inspiration fuels innovation.

With your core message coming to light, you can bring all of your expertise together under one umbrella to begin your own process of innovation. In choosing to see the forest instead of only the trees, you open yourself up to so many more possibilities. You can explore how different subjects intertwine, feed off one another, and can improve by looking at the way things are done in other areas. This is the spark that can lead to incredible strides in your work. The best part about it is that the umbrella you create with your core message will serve as the focus you need in your business and alleviate the need for a much smaller niche—thus freeing you up to continue seeing the bigger picture (i.e., the forest) instead of only putting your head down to see the details of the trees (i.e., one focus area).

Let's be clear for a minute here on the importance of focus. You will need a prime focus to be successful in business. There's no denying that. Without it, you'll be lost in the weeds, not knowing where you're headed and confusing the people who actually could use your help. They wouldn't even know they needed you if you were unclear about what value you provided to them. However, with focus, it can become clear to you as the entrepreneur what you're trying to accomplish and how you can be of value to the world. Plus, it becomes clear to those who are waiting for someone like you as to how you can help them see differently or make the changes that they so desperately need to make.

As we discussed earlier, your core message will give you this focus in a different way than a niche can because it will still allow you freedom of choice when it comes to the work you put out into the world. It frees you up to be without limitation in how you deliver your message. One day you may decide to write a book, and the next you may choose to do an art show, teach a local class, or even open an online store. Those are all different niches and business types that many experts would tell you require specialization in the areas of writing, art, instruction, or even sales. Whereas, with the methodology of a core theme or message, you can do all of those things, and do them quite well. You'll just be creating your expert status around your core message instead of the specialized type of work.

This is how good a core message can be for a multi-passionate brand. It helps you to shape the forest rather than only work around the trees. Quite a different perspective on business-building now, isn't it? I would wager to say that this way of establishing a personal brand is what many will eventually be headed toward in future careers. After all, the business landscape and the way people buy is quickly changing in this technological age. We no longer feel pressed to work with large-scale companies that don't have a personal relationship or genuine connection with us but are solely present to sell. So the real question becomes whether you can become an expert in the marketplace when you do a variety of things. From the perspective of having a core driving message that defines everything you do, I would give that a resounding 'yes.'

When it comes to the positioning of your business, however, it will require you to reframe the way you structure your business to be either a personal brand or to be a business centered around a unique, multi-dimensional experience. The personal brand would be the one more structured upon a portfolio or body of work whereas creating an experiential business would cater to one or two primary expertise areas with your other interests serving to create a unique experience for customers. More on this in later chapters, but for now, all you have to do is understand that what you once thought of as a niche can easily be reframed as your core message or unifying theme. Get that straight, and you'll have the beginning of a clear and focused yet flexible business.

I want to make it easier for you to understand the possibilities for your multi-passionate business, so it's important to run through some real, tangible examples here. The examples I'll present here are businesses on a variety of different levels from large to small. Some are brands that the majority of us know well while others may be running successfully in small markets that aren't seen in the larger public eye. Let's start with a few bigger names that you already probably know, and then we'll work our way down to some smaller influencers that can still serve as great examples. Once you see the variety, I think you'll have a better understanding of how you can establish your own success on any level you choose.

Now, there are a few well-known entrepreneurs that will help to get us on the same page to start with here. Don't be intimidated by the size of their success. These examples in no way, shape, or form dictate what you should aspire to in your own business. They'll merely help you to think big initially and help me to demonstrate what we're talking about in terms of unifying themes to their work. However, a lot of times when we do think of prolific entrepreneurs who do multiple types of work, we immediately come up with celebrities and famous people. They're easy examples for us all to draw from, and those are the people in our society who have really become massive personal brands we all know immediately.

First, look at celebrity entrepreneur, Martha Stewart. She found success and grew an incredible business all from the roots of being a caterer.[17] With her knack for style and handmade touches, Martha put a homemade spin on all the things she would do to make them special. She got her start in catering, applied a unifying theme of creating memorable experiences through personalized touches and was able to broaden her reach to grow a

---

[17] Biography.com Editors. (2014, April 2). Martha Stewart Biography. Retrieved from https://www.biography.com/people/martha-stewart-9542234

multi-faceted business reaching millions daily. Now, not only does the Martha Stewart brand cover cooking, but it also branches into event planning, weddings, handmade projects, family activities, and even holiday decor and interior design...All because she had the vision and insight to start with her unifying theme and expand into many areas that made sense along with it.[18]

What about the incredible genius of serial entrepreneur, Elon Musk? With a relentless drive for knowledge and an undeniable hope to make the world a better place, Elon made it a goal of his to be an innovator from an early age.[19] He knew that by combining areas of expertise, he could create innovation in disciplines key to our advancement. That meant honing in on many of his interests in technology, computer interaction, space travel, and energy to develop new ways of thinking and approaching our world.[20] His interdisciplinary approach

---

[18] Biography.com Editors. (2014, April 2). Martha Stewart Biography. Retrieved from https://www.biography.com/people/martha-stewart-9542234
[19] Biography.com Editors. (2014. April 2). Elon Musk Biography. Retrieved from https://www.biography.com/people/elon-musk-20837159
[20] The Infographic.ly Team. (2017, Feb 9). "Infographic: Elon Musk - Profile Of A Prolific Entrepreneur." Retrieved from https://www.entrepreneur.com/article/288904

to these areas has allowed for numerous advancements and the openness to new possibilities in these fields.[21]

The actor, George Clooney, is another example of a multi-faceted entrepreneur. He's a very well-known actor, but he's also a filmmaker, political and economic activist, non-profit organizer and chairperson, advocate for humanitarianism, and a resolution advocate for the conflict in Darfur.[22] The acting roles that he chooses are centered around impactful issues in society, and he's garnered high acclaim for those roles. Clooney has now chosen to use his publicity and stature to advocate for other causes that matter most to him, thus positioning himself as an activist for positive change in the world.[23]

Jessica Alba is not quite as well known as the first few. However, she is a celebrity that many are familiar with through her movies. She's an actress, author, activist, advocate for sustainable family living, and now a natural baby care product creator.[24] Her innate tendencies

---

[21] Biography.com Editors. (2014. April 2). Elon Musk Biography. Retrieved from https://www.biography.com/people/elon-musk-20837159

[22] Wikipedia.com. (2018, November 15). "George Clooney." Retrieved from https://en.wikipedia.org/wiki/George_Clooney

[23] Wikipedia.com. (2018, November 15). "George Clooney." Retrieved from https://en.wikipedia.org/wiki/George_Clooney

[24] Griffith, Kathleen. (2018, June 29). "Jessica Alba on Being Brave, Dealing With Self-Doubt and Overcoming Major

toward entrepreneurship have allowed her to intertwine her passions into a body of work focused around living a balanced life of health and wellbeing. While she's known for being an actress first, her work branched out into multiple platforms and business models to make the impact she wanted to make in the world.[25]

When you look at celebrities and big names in their industries, you could say that it all came easily for them as they received fame and notoriety first before branching out. However, if we peel back the layers, we see that may only be true in select cases. In reality, many well-known entrepreneurs probably had a big vision to start with and most likely understood that in order to build that vision, they would need to have a clear focus regarding everything they did. This is where that overarching theme and core message really starts coming into play. It's something that you can determine from the very beginning and use to define what you want to be known for in all of your life's work. It's your legacy.

You as a rising multi-passionate entrepreneur can use these examples as inspiration for building your own focused legacy as well. Allow it to shape the important work that you must do in the world to get that message

---

Breakdowns." Retrieved from https://www.entrepreneur.com/article/315948

[25] Griffith, Kathleen. (2018, June 29). "Jessica Alba on Being Brave, Dealing With Self-Doubt and Overcoming Major Breakdowns." Retrieved from https://www.entrepreneur.com/article/315948

across and make big changes. This is the ultimate cata-
pult for your creativity and inspiration because there are
no limits to what you can achieve. You're only bounded
by your own mindset and beliefs, which hopefully we
dispelled most of in the previous chapter. The decision
to make now is whether you'll accept this important
work as your purpose and move forward with getting
your message out.

Just in case you might be a little taken aback by the
intensity of those first few examples I provided, I'll give
you a few more on a different scale. Hopefully, these will
be a bit easier for you to relate to as I go through each
one. After all, when you're just starting out it can be
much more comforting to see people closer to where you
are achieving success that doesn't seem so far away or
unachievable. It also helps to be mindful of where these
people were when they were first starting out. Although
the media makes it seem so, they didn't become success
stories overnight. It took years for them to get where
they are now, and you have to look at the whole picture
of their journey for it to make sense in context.

Now, on a scale that's not so massive as the first few
examples, we can first identify, Marie Forleo, the woman
behind the term "multi-passionate entrepreneur."[26]

---

[26] Feloni, Richard and Myelle Lansat. (2018, August 20). "A
business coach who's taught thousands of people explains why
it's OK to be a jack-of-all-trades instead of knowing exactly
what you want to do." Retrieved from https://

Although there have been several others before her who used terms such as scanner or renaissance soul, she was the self-proclaimed multi-passionate person who started using the phrase to describe her multifaceted entrepreneurial spirit. Marie is a very well-known life coach, founder of the B-School community, author, dance and fitness instructor, fashion lover, and more.[27] Over the years she has gone from one passion to another, ultimately choosing to create more of an experiential business focused first on life coaching with other passions complimenting that primary expertise. She adds in her love of fashion, dance and humor to the videos and skits she does for her YouTube channel.[28] Her interest in the human story and lifelong learning is evident in the interviews she does with other influential entrepreneurs and creatives. Plus, she's not afraid to add in a bit of her spiritual thinking to the mix when the support her audience needs calls for it. By combining much of what she loves into her brand experience, Marie not only has the flexibility of how she shows up for her tribe as who she

---

www.businessinsider.com/business-coach-marie-forleo-career-advice-2018-8

[27] Feloni, Richard and Myelle Lansat. (2018, August 20). "A business coach who's taught thousands of people explains why it's OK to be a jack-of-all-trades instead of knowing exactly what you want to do." Retrieved from https://www.businessinsider.com/business-coach-marie-forleo-career-advice-2018-8

[28] Forleo, Marie. (2018). "Marie TV: Create a Business and Life You Love." Retrieved from https://www.youtube.com/user/marieforleo

truly is but also to quickly build her know, like, and trust factor to genuinely connect with the people in her community.

Tim Ferris is another great example of a multi-passionate entrepreneur focused on self-improvement and empowerment in business and life. As an author, interviewer, podcaster, startup business investor, and more, Ferris embraces his life as a jack-of-all-trades and emphasizes the importance of interconnection among many different disciplines.[29] He advocates for the 80/20 rule when looking at how much of a subject you need to be proficient in order to become an expert.[30] Just as we discussed previously, you can learn a great deal on a subject so that you know the truly integral parts of it (maybe about 50-70% of its basis), and then you can easily move on knowing you have enough knowledge to be incredibly valuable in that subject.

Tim even goes as far on his blog as to say, "The specialist who imprisons himself in self-inflicted one-dimensionality- pursuing an impossible perfection- spends decades stagnant or making imperceptible incremental improvements while the curious generalist consistently measures

---

[29] Ferriss, Tim. (2007, September 14). "The Top 5 Reasons to Be a Jack of All Trades." Retrieved from https://tim.blog/2007/09/14/the-top-5-reasons-to-be-a-jack-of-all-trades/
[30] Ferriss, Tim. (2007, September 14). "The Top 5 Reasons to Be a Jack of All Trades." Retrieved from https://tim.blog/2007/09/14/the-top-5-reasons-to-be-a-jack-of-all-trades/

improvement in quantum leaps. It is only the latter who enjoys the process of pursuing excellence."[31] So in saying this, Ferris believes strongly in the greater potential of multi-passionates to build meaningful careers than that of people honing in on one thing for a lifetime. Not only that, but because you're able to make quick strides and happily pursue your choice of disciplines, you'll find much more joy along the way. How's that for the blessing of someone who's been there, done that, and generated the millions of dollars to show for it?

That's definitely one intense take on multi-passionate career-building. What about something more relatable to the everyday person, though? It just so happens that I've got a few of those examples for you as well. First off, I want to introduce you to successful blogger and writer, Jeff Goins, who started in a non-profit career field.[32] You may know his books, *The Art of Work*, *You are a Writer*, and *Real Artists Don't Starve*, to name a few. Goins found his passion for writing by accident at the suggestion of a friend. Since starting his authorship career, he has since branched off into further passions that compliment his writing. Those include event and workshop planning and also marketing through storytelling. Jeff has discov-

---

[31] Ferriss, Tim. (2007, September 14). "The Top 5 Reasons to Be a Jack of All Trades." Retrieved from https://tim.blog/2007/09/14/the-top-5-reasons-to-be-a-jack-of-all-trades/
[32] Goins, Jeff. (2015). "The Importance of Changing Mediums: Why We Need More Polymaths in the 21st Century." Retrieved from https://goinswriter.com/change-medium/

ered that mastering a few interest areas and connecting them in a congruent way can really help you to never stop growing.[33]

Taking a look at another creative, we can see that Kari Chapin is all about handmade business.[34] She is the author of three books on the subject, teaches courses for Creative Live on running handmade businesses, consults for small businesses, gives motivational speeches, and hosts her own podcast.[35] Chapin has essentially built a successful career doing a plethora of projects all around the unifying theme of creative, handmade entrepreneurship. When you go to her website, it's clear that she's established herself as a personal brand, and the feeling around everything she does is a playful and artistic vibe.[36] So for those who choose to work with her in any capacity, they'll know that's the approach they'll get to the services she provides.

Last but certainly not least, we have Sally Hope, a life coach at the Wildheart Revolution. Sally is a constant

---

[33] Goins, Jeff. (2015). "The Importance of Changing Mediums: Why We Need More Polymaths in the 21st Century." Retrieved from https://goinswriter.com/change-medium/

[34] Chapin, Kari. (2018). Retrieved from https://www.karichapin.com/

[35] Chapin, Kari. (2018). "Offers These Services." Retrieved from https://www.karichapin.com/offers-these-services/

[36] Chapin. Kari. (2018). "Home." Retrieved from https://www.karichapin.com/

traveler, an RV-er, a previous rock band member, a Facebook community manager for Marie Forleo's B-School, and so much more.[37] She's managed to find the intersection among her passions to where she can help people live exactly the way they want. Sally is a great example of a multi-passionate person with a business model focused on a primary expertise area as the heart of her offers. Then, she uses her complimentary passions as well as her personality to create a unique approach and experience for her clients. If you go to her website, you can see how she's intertwined them into her growing coaching business that serves people who resonate with her approach the most.[38]

This is only the beginning of seeing multi-passionates at work in our society. We haven't even covered examples of those who have lived in decades or even centuries past, especially during the Renaissance period. During that time, it was very highly regarded to be well-versed in several disciplines. It's only through the way that time and culture have shaped our work lives that we've found ourselves in a place where being multifaceted is seen as a bit of a second class. However, now is the time for a new awakening on this subject. The newest generation is telling us that they refuse to settle for careers that put them in a box. The right mindset to create innova-

[37] Hope, Sally. (2018). "Hey, I'm Sally." Retrieved from https://sallyhope.com/about-sally/
[38] Hope, Sally. (2018). "Homepage." Retrieved from https://sallyhope.com/

tion is emerging again. It's the moment where we need to listen more to what's inside of us and do the work that must come out rather than what's expected.

Each of the people we've discussed in this section has taken a different approach to his or her business and career. Some have chosen to be lifelong learners or artists or utilize the structure of a traditional business model that they enhance. In the coming chapters, I'm going to show you how to decide the best approach for you. I'll give you examples of how to lend more structure to your endeavors and stay focused even in the face of that nagging internal clock. First, though, we need to address what's at the heart of it all for you. Just as each of these people has found a way to connect their areas of expertise, you can as well once you find what ties it all together. That's where it all begins and the place where you'll always want to find your way back to no matter what you choose to do.

Finding the reasoning behind all that you do can be a challenge, and it may or may not already be apparent to you. In the action exercise in this chapter, you did some brainstorming as to how to categorize your areas of interest and find the theme that ties them all together. If you found a specific unifying theme, then you're ready to put it into practice. If not, then I have a couple more questions for you to consider before we discuss implementing your core message. They both have to do with what you would say if you only had a brief moment to talk to your ideal audience on a massive scale. They shouldn't be things that you have to think about for an extended period of time but rather should naturally come to the top of your mind right away.

First, think about if you were to walk up onto a stage in front of a massive audience and only have five minutes to speak. What is the one thing that you would have to say to them? There's probably something that comes to you immediately that you inherently know you want to say. Now, alternately, you can ask yourself this question in a different light. What if you had a billboard in the middle of a large world city that masses of people could see and read as they passed? Think about the most important message that you'd absolutely have to get out there into the world and know it would reach millions. What would it be? Your message should come from your gut as an instinctual, undeniable piece of advice, knowledge, motivation, or plea. The more heartfelt and sincere it is and the more it relates to what you believe, the better.

For example, you may have a sense that if you were on stage, the biggest message you would have would be that love and family are the most important things in life. To someone else, it would be imperative to advocate for taking care of ourselves physically, and yet another person may believe in the power communication to promote connection in this world. Each of these perspectives is incredibly powerful and valid in their own right.

Look at your own responses to both of those scenarios. Are they similar or identifiably tangential? There's probably something connecting them for you. You may need to make some refinements to those messages in order for them to make sense together in conjunction with your passions. As long as it feels like your responses came from your heart and speak to what you value, you're on the right track.

There are a lot of coaches out there who will tell you that you need to keep drilling down further and further with what you do until you hit a very specific niche. As a multi-passionate person, I've found that it's better to leave it a bit broad at first until you figure out whether being more specific will serve you well. You may find that you get bored with teaching one aspect of your message or don't want to approach your message from a certain angle. That's okay, but you won't know that until you try things out. Give it some time and allow yourself to be open to whatever fits your message for the time being. This will help you feel less constrained about what you can and can't do as you navigate how to set up your business to keep you fulfilled. All you need to make sure of is that your message is specific to what you value and stand for overall. That'll be the thing that draws other people to you and your work as they value the same things and want to be a part of what you do.

As far as how these internal beliefs relate to the business you want to grow, you must understand that it all starts from what you stand for in the world. It's almost like the purpose that we usually associate with finding our calling. We've each been given our strengths and talents to go along with this belief and core message. We all have backgrounds and experiences that we've been through for a reason. If you can find a way to use your unique expertise and experiences to further your positive message in the world, then think about how much of an impact you could make.

On a larger scale, can you see how if each person advocated for their own positive core message and used their unique talents to be of service how much better of a world we would live in? Instead of stove-piping everyone into single-focus jobs out of necessity, each one of us could be embracing all that we've been given and using it for the greater good. This is something that good human resources managers know already. You have to use your resources wisely. When it comes to people, knowing their skills and talents and using them effectively could mean the difference between an effective, successful organization and one that stays stagnant without growth. The same goes for our society and whether we choose to embrace the multi-talented abilities of those within our communities to activate growth and positive change. Tapping into our core beliefs along with our unique strengths gives us the perfect opportunity to do this.

Planning out your message in your head is one thing, but relating it to an audience is another. So, how do you use your core message in your business and convey it to your audience through your content and platform? Well, for one thing, branding and marketing are all about getting your big message across on a continual basis. It's what everything you do revolves around. Take the Disney brand as an example. Their core message is centered around bringing your dreams to life.[39] They use a magical brand archetype to do this, and every piece of marketing material they put out or product they create is focused around this inherent driver of bringing dreams to life. It's become such an emotional message that really gets people of all ages to enjoy their brand because of the magic they bring into everything they do.[40]

For someone like you who is multi-passionate, your core message can also become the driver of your entire brand. It can shape the free content you put out, what you post on social media, the paid offers and services you create, and even the entire way you interact with your audience. Just as Disney has done with creating a customer experience, you can also establish a feeling that connects your core message to what your audience

---

[39] Gabor, Deb. (2017, May 25). "Twelve Brand Archetypes-Which is Yours?" Retrieved from http://www.cobizmag.com/Business-Insights/The-12-brand-archetypes--Which-is-yours/
[40] Brand Personalities. (2018). "The Magician." Retrieved from https://brandpersonalities.com.au/personalities/the-magician/

hopes for. Your brand then becomes synonymous with what your audience idealizes and holds dear to them as they aspire to change, grow, or solve their problems. It may be a feeling of admiration and love if you're family-oriented. It may be a feeling of artistry and sophistication if you're focused on beauty in the world. The bottom line is that connecting your message to your audience requires a feeling that carries through in everything you do.

In later chapters, I'll go deeper into creating a feeling for your brand. For now, I want to make sure that you've identified your audience, or the people who need your message the most and who you'd like to work with the most. It may be more than just one category of people, and that's perfectly fine. It's important, though, to focus on groups that could use your message in their lives and need your particular approach to it to give them the solution they need.

When you develop the work you do based on a core driving message or theme, it's likely that you'll have to segment your audience. This will either be because as we said you'll appeal to more than one type of person or your work will be so diverse that it'll pertain to various needs. Ryan Levesque, the founder of the Ask Method, equates this approach to organizing Legos, something many parents struggle with when their little ones get really interested in the building kits.[41] Ryan mentions on his blog that throwing all of the Lego pieces together into one big bucket is not the answer, just as combining all of your audience into one shouldn't be either.

He instead recommends sorting them according to certain categories or needs. While this might be color, size, or type for Legos, when it comes to your audience, it could mean anything from what format people are interested in hearing their information in to whether they prefer your cooking content over your workout content. So each category of people may show up because they love your core message and what you stand for, but they're all interested in implementing it in their own ways. When you segment them into clear, manageable categories, it becomes that much easier to deliver exactly what they need and want and make them feel like you're speaking directly to them.[42]

Don't get me wrong on this point, though. You don't have to have more than one type of audience. It just depends on how you choose to approach your work. If you don't fall into that camp, then you'll want to be very

[41] Levesque, Ryan. (2017). "The "LEGO Secret" to Generate More Leads & Customers (Part 1 of 3)." Retrieved from http:// askmethod.com/blog/the-secret-to-profitably-growing-your-list-part-1-of-3/

[42] Levesque, Ryan. (2017). "The "LEGO Secret" to Generate More Leads & Customers (Part 1 of 3)." Retrieved from http:// askmethod.com/blog/the-secret-to-profitably-growing-your-list-part-1-of-3/

specific about choosing the group of people that you want to work with and who really needs you. It'll take a while to test out working with several people and getting a feel for each. It may turn out that you love the variety in who you work with, or it may be that you know exactly who you connect with right from the beginning. Be open to the possibilities on this, and let your instinct be your guide as to whether someone is a good fit or not.

This is another area where many people will tell you that you absolutely need to have a very small, select ideal audience type in order to be successful. I'm going to let you be the judge about whether that's right for you or not, though, because it all depends on the business model you create. If you choose to create a personal brand with a broader approach to your work, then you'll want to use the segmentation method with a variety of audience types. If you have a primary area of expertise that you create your business around, then yes, honing in on a select group of people will probably serve you best. It's all relative to the way you want to build your business, and there's no wrong way unless you don't understand why you're making your choice one way or the other.

The goal when choosing your audience is so that you know who you're talking to and so that you can speak directly to their needs and wants. When you have a focus around a core message, that message will be the thing that weeds people out for you. It'll do the job of making it clear who you fit with and who you won't.

You don't want to try to reach everyone. That's the easiest way to fall flat and have your message get lost on deaf ears. However, if you're clear enough about what exactly you represent, believe in, and value, then that will bring the right people to you. They'll start to find you online and in the marketplace by the content you're creating around that message, and it will seem like you're speaking right to them because they believe in the same things.

Let's take a look at a couple examples of this. You may be all about family bonding experiences as your core message, so your work includes family travel blogging, being a family therapist, and even writing books on fun activities for kids. Even though it may seem like families are your target market, you most likely have three different audiences with different needs. Some parents may be interested in learning how to save on a family vacation through your blog. Others will need your support in person as a therapist when they're going through tough times. Yet, with your books you may be targeting moms specifically who spend their days at home with their small children. When you market yourself to those audiences, you'll likely be using very different language for each one. However, when they find you in the beginning, they may all be drawn to you from your overall message of family bonding and creating experiences together.

Here's another one. You may be interested in teaching people to have a strong foundation in business, and you draw on your education in finance and marketing in your offers. You decide to create an umbrella company focused on business fundamentals and include a variety of offers under this overarching company idea. First, you create an online course to help new small business owners figure out how to set up their bookkeeping and accounting systems. You may also realize that part of that strong foundation you advocate for is marketing, so you create a YouTube channel to talk about marketing strategies for bloggers. In addition to those, you may decide that you want to open an online store that sells digital business plan templates for creatives that have a hard time with the systems in their businesses. Each one of these can be a business in its own right. Yet, you've managed to successfully integrate them under your umbrella of business fundamentals, and you've got the expertise in each of those areas to back them all up. Now this means, though, that you've got several different audience types that you're catering to in your business: start-up business owners, bloggers needing marketing advice, and creatives needing a business plan. You'll have to be extremely diligent in segmenting each one here, but it's doable. You would just need to be mindful of first addressing your overarching idea of having a strong business foundation and then being careful of how you speak to each group's pain points after that.

These examples are just meant to show you the possibility of providing offerings to more than one target audience. This method is complicated for sure and would require specific launch phases with careful planning in order to work. It's not something that you would build fully in even a year. By no means is this the easiest way to build up a following and a tribe, but it is doable if you want to create a variety of things. I'm highlighting it here only to give you the concept around how you can cater to multiple audience types. The more specific you are with who you serve, though, the better. It's just that when you're multi-passionate and your life's work is not drilled down to solely one thing, you've got to allow yourself some grace and flexibility. The segmentation method can provide a way to do that if you're diligent about keeping your tribe's interests and needs organized within the backend of your business systems.

Having said that working with multiple target audiences is doable, I do want to back up a bit and be clear about where your starting point should be here. First and foremost, start with simplicity. Test out each audience type before committing to any specific one, and along the same lines, give yourself the ability to start with just one offer to just one target audience. Yes, it's hard to do one thing at a time, but when you're starting something new, it's imperative. This is the one time where I will tell you that focus on a specific task is undeniably required: in the beginning stages of a new project. As you develop your new offering, you'll get a feel for whether it makes sense to market it to more than one audience or not. It may be only natural, but you've got to keep things as simple as possible in the beginning to know for sure.

Remember when you were in science class in elementary school? When you started learning about how to create an experiment, the teacher would instruct you to keep the variables to a minimum so that it would be clear what effect each one had on the result. Otherwise, it would be too difficult to determine which variable actually created the outcome you observed. You can apply this same principle to the beginning stages of your business, especially in terms of the critical components like your audience. You want to start with one target, see if your offer resonates with them, and build off of that. If it doesn't feel right or the results aren't there, then move to the next and test that one out. The same goes for adding more offers to the mix. As in our last example of the company focused on strong business foundations, you would want to only start with the online bookkeeping course first. Then, you could branch off to the YouTube channel and online store later.

That doesn't mean that you have to only do one thing for an extended period of time. Your internal multi-passionate clock will definitely go off if you do that! What it does mean, though, is that you should give yourself some time for testing and building momentum. You can decide the right amount of time for that based on your own needs, but this is the best way to set yourself up for success in the beginning stages. So tell yourself that you're going to allow for one month, one quarter, or even six months if that works for you. Then, make the proper pivots as you go and continue branching out when the time feels right.

The other thing that will be an incredible help to you in the beginning stages of starting a new venture is to have a specific ideal customer in mind. Now, you may be saying, "I thought you just told me that I didn't have to have a specific customer in mind?" Well, yes and no. Yes, you do need to specify someone in your own mind so that you have a reference point when you're creating your content. No, you don't have to always cater to that one person only. Let's clarify this distinction so it makes a bit more sense. Since we just went over how you can have more than one type of audience, that part should be apparent. However, when I say that you should have an ideal customer in mind, I'm talking about making it easier for you as the content creator as well as for the people who need to find you.

You can make it easier on yourself by creating what's known as a customer avatar. This can be based on a real person or one that you've made up in your mind to be ideal for you. You outline all of their needs, wants, likes, dislikes, typical day, pain points, and what they wish they had in their lives. Knowing these things makes it so much easier on you as the content creator to be able to speak to that person in your writing, create images and videos for that person, and also to establish offers that support them in their needs. On the flip side, you're making it easier on your ideal customer as well when you do this. By clearly laying out ways that you cater to their values, ideals, beliefs, and pain points, they can more clearly see how you're perfect for them. When you use the same words that they use to describe their feelings and issues, it's as if you're reading their mind, and they'll instantly connect with what you're saying to them.

In addition, you may have multiple ideal customer avatars. Just as when you have multiple offers or products you're creating, you'll also have multiple ideal customers that suit each of those categories. Take our previous example of the family bonding work. From the category of people who are interested in family travel, you may come up with an ideal customer avatar who is a mom to three elementary school kids, on a budget for one trip per year, and who's very interested in international experiences that give the kids a cultural education as well as a fun adventure. Your second ideal customer avatar would come from the category of those needing a family therapist, and you may identify that person as someone you actually know who is a working mother, lacking on time for her family, but determined to make the most of the time she does have with her two kids and her husband on the weekends. So you've got two very specific customer avatars that you use in different areas of your business based on individual needs.

These customer avatars don't in any way confine you to serving only people similar to your avatar. You are simply using them to make your life easier as you market and use relational language, but from there you can ease up on who you work with if you'd like. This is what I mean when I say that you don't have to cater to one specific person necessarily. You just want to have a connection point to relate to your customers as you market and create offerings, and that's the biggest reason that you choose a customer avatar and specific audience. Perhaps someone else walks in the door that doesn't fit into those categories. Yet, they still need your help, and you're willing to work with them. Then, by all means, go for it! You want to set yourself up for ease but not limitations. Only utilize the customer avatars, and any constraints in your business for that matter, up until the point that it makes your decision-making easier. After that, open yourself up to whatever possibilities come your way.

Action Exercise:

Figure out your ideal customer avatar by asking yourself some very important questions that are outlined here. Do this exercise for each specific category of people you plan to work with so that you can directly speak to their individual needs with your content.

The first thing to work on is how you bridge across all of the people that need your message. There will be a common language and way of presenting your content that resonates with them all. This will be what you use to find those who believe the same thing that you believe and resonate with you as the person behind the brand. Use this on your homepage, your tag lines, and even in speeches that you give to weed people out when they're just finding you.

First, to determine the audience for your larger message, ask yourself these questions:

1. What groups of people need your core message?
2. What groups of people do you currently belong to or who do you have the most in common with?
3. What are the issues or common pain points around your message or unifying theme that are consistent across all the people you can help?
4. Is there common language that you can use to show all of these people that you understand what they need or want?

Next, answer the following questions for every group of people that you plan to work within your business. Use each one as you develop the content geared specifically for their pain points.

For your specific work, services, or products:

1. In what format do you most like to present my work (i.e. one on one, groups, podcast, video, course, webinar, books, etc.)?
2. What types of people are drawn to that format of learning?
3. Is there a specific group of people who would bene-fit most from your work in a particular area?

For each ideal customer avatar: (You may only have one, especially in the beginning.)

1. What is their pain point?
2. How does this relate to your core message or unifying theme around your work?
3. What specific language do they use to talk about their issues?
4. What do they feel like right now?
5. Where do they want to eventually be once their problem is solved?
6. How can you relate to them right now through your experiences, background, personality, or life stories?
7. What expertise, strengths, or knowledge do you have that they will find beneficial?

List out the qualities of your customer avatar as if they are a person you already know (or maybe they are!):

1. What is his or her name?
2. What is their family situation, marital status, and home life like?
3. What is their financial situation?
4. Do they have organizations they like or communities where they can be found?
5. What books or other media do they consume? (Be specific about what they like, listen to, watch, etc).
6. Name other people that they follow for advice or as guides, instructors, coaches, and influencers.
7. Determine the top three places where you can interact with this person.

Once you have determined your ideal customer base and avatars, you can use those to tailor the language you use in your marketing copy as well as to make your offerings specific to their needs. This will give you the

ability to reach your audience on a much deeper level
than if you were just trying to talk to everyone.

Going a bit deeper here into how you actually create
content that talks to your ideal customers, I want to give
you a framework for where to start. You know you need
to keep things as simple as possible and also use your
ideal customer avatars to get specific. So as you sit down
to create your website, write your blog posts or when
you are thinking about what images to capture for your
social media, you need to have a plan in your mind for
tailoring it to your audience. An easy way to approach
this is to start by communicating with your entire audience first based on your core message, and then to be
more specific as people funnel further into your
business.

When someone first finds your business, where will they
be? Most likely, they'll be on your website or social
media if online. It may be through an interview, speech,
or introduction from someone else. This is the perfect
opportunity to approach them with your core
messaging. Use language that connects all the people
you can help. Find the intersection of what they're all
looking for and use that as a starting point. For instance,
if you are a photographer that's passionate about integrating many artistic mediums, you may talk about
combining photography with styling, architecture, and
even cooking. People who may be drawn to your work

could include food bloggers, a local chamber of commerce, and restaurant owners. Each of them could resonate with the images and copy you use on your website as a whole, but individually, they each have their own agenda as to why they need your services. They'll dive deeper into the services or products they need the most from you, and that's where you focus on resonating with them separately.

You should reference your core message in all of your content no matter where that is. Let's say you have a podcast. So in the intro audio of the podcast where you introduce your show and what you talk about, your core message needs to be clear. This is where you want to bridge across the specific customer avatars that you have and use the language that will make your message hit home for them equally, just as you would do on your website homepage. Then, after that, you may have key components of your message that are tailored to each avatar. Those are your content pillars, or the set of content subjects that you talk about regularly, and it's perfectly fine for those to be more tailored. When you get to that point, it'll be within certain podcast episodes, blog posts, freebies, or paid offers you create.

Let's walk through how you would do this for one customer avatar first. Cold traffic includes people who are seeing your business for the first time. These people will come to your website homepage, about page, social media profiles, YouTube channel, and listen to any interviews or podcast episodes with you in them. In these places, you want to touch on your core message as well as hit on specific content pillars that pertain to your customer's pain points. Then, as people start to follow you and see more from your brand, you start to funnel them through your free content such as free workbooks and videos, email content, checklists, or anything else you're providing in exchange for an email address. This is where they truly enter what's called your sales funnel. On this level, you should focus attention on one of their pain points and speak directly to their concerns. Then, when you get to your paid programs, products, and services, you should be playing into your customer's hierarchy of needs to hit on their ultimate pain point. This is where specific language and stories that allow you to relate to them are critical.

Now when you have more than one customer avatar, you'll need to adjust how you communicate at each of these levels slightly. When people just start finding you, it's important to connect to all of the people who'll res-onate with your message so that you can segregate them into lists in the next step. You can first give them insight into your broad message and a taste of your content pillars that pertain to individual pain points. Once you get to the point that you're providing them with specific free content, that's when you start to segregate your audience and allow for greater individualization in your language and content. Finally, when you get down to offering your paid products and services, you'll be doing the same thing that you would with only one customer avatar: you will approach your customers with specific language tailored solely to their individual issue to show them that you understand where they're coming from.

That should give you a better understanding of how you cater to one versus many customer types. With multiple customer types, as you funnel people through your content, you'll have more tailored content. This will keep you more organized and allow you to talk directly to all of your customers' needs. Remember, though, that you want to start simply and cater to one customer avatar at a time. Otherwise, you'll run the risk of burning out and stretching yourself too thin. If you've only got one ideal customer avatar, then you're golden. You can just focus on that one avatar for all of your offers and content, regardless of what stage of your funnel the person happens to be in at the moment.

The most important way you can stand out to the right people with the content and offers you create is to be specific about what you believe in, value, and idealize. If you can do this at even the highest levels of your sales funnel when people are just started to get to know your business, that will allow you to make your message very cohesive and consistent. Your ideal audience will hone in on you in the larger, crowded marketplace because you'll be the one saying exactly what they're thinking, what they're feeling, and what they hope for as well. You'll be the one who's doing it on a consistent basis, drilling home the message they need to hear in ways that make the most sense to them.

This is so much easier said than done, though, and can really be the topic of a whole other book. You need to be extremely mindful of tying everything together and being consistent. That is how your brand will make sense in your mind and in the minds of your customers. If you have that unifying theme, the cohesiveness is there for you already. You just have to use it to guide all that you do and create. With that in mind, you can shape your copy, your images, your promotions, and everything in between to reflect that cohesive message.

In addition to keeping things simple, knowing your customer avatars, and consistently referencing your core message, you must also show your audience the value in what you do. When I say show them, I'm talking about not only telling them, but actually illustrating it for them. Many times a message or lesson doesn't completely click for us until we can actually see it in action. This may mean painting a picture with a story, using an image, or creating a video. Whatever it may be for you, it helps to solidify the value you bring to your audience when you can give them something tangible to latch onto. That way it'll be much easier for them to see what's possible and how they, too, can make a change that's needed in their lives.

When it comes to doing this in your content, it can be as straightforward as posting an image on social of how you have the freedom to work on your laptop at the beach. Alternately, you could show review videos about how a line of bath products you created will help your customers to relax and get rid of the stress in their lives. It's all relative to the need that your audience has deep down and the platform by which you can reach them most effectively. It's up to you to figure out how to merge those two in a way that makes sense for your business. Once you find one or two ways to get your value across and make an impact on your audience, stick with those consistently and put your energy toward what works.

As you can see, core messaging will help you to clarify your objectives in everything you do as well as to resonate more fully with the people who need your work. Whether you've realized it previously or not, there is a commonality in all of your interests and passions. Once you determine what that is, it'll be like a switch flipped on inside your head, and you'll be able to see how it all makes sense together. First, get it clear for yourself. Then, get it clear for your audience.

We've gone through some pretty incredible examples of how other entrepreneurs have put this together for themselves. Now it's up to you to do the same because your message is far greater than yourself. People are waiting for you and the approach you have to your work. They're hoping they'll find someone who can deliver the message they need exactly the way you can, even if they only know it subconsciously right now. The only way to start owning your gifts and showing up for

them is to acknowledge this big message that's inside of you and let it come out in whatever ways it needs to manifest. Give it a try. Do the work. Embrace the fact that your
audience needs your specific voice, and dare to show up for them to hear you.

Chapter Five

Determining Your Entrepreneurial Role

There are so many different ways to present your natural talents and gifts to the world. What may be the right method for you may not be for someone else. To identify what will work best for you, it's a good idea to look at the way you innately approach the things you do. I'm not talking about whether you like to write or take pictures. Instead, in this chapter, I want you to think about the role you want to play in society as you do your work. Do you want to be an advocate? Do you want to take charge? Do you want to be a creator?

All of these questions revolve around the entrepreneurial role that you most identify with naturally. In essence, this is how you can position yourself as the change-maker you're meant to be. Whether you're thinking about writing a book, opening an online store, or creating a coaching business, you can gain a lot of insight into the path you should take by first understanding the bigger role you play in relation to your tribe. Dumbing it down a bit, think about it as if you're choosing whether you want to be a Steve Jobs, a Leonardo DaVinci, a Deepak Chopra, a Dr. Martin Luther King, Jr., or an Oprah Winfrey.

Each of those people carry or have carried a variety of different talents and capabilities within them. Yet, they each chose to wield those capabilities in specific ways suited best to them. Steve Jobs was an incredible innovator. His work integrated multiple fields to create major breakthroughs in the field of technology. Leonardo DaVinci was a creative whose work in a broad range of fields has allowed people for hundreds of years to see the world in greater depth.[43] Deepak Chopra is a thought leader who speaks to the masses about spiritual growth and balancing the mind, body, and spirit. He uses platforms of authorship, speaking engagements, and workshops to change people's perceptions about their world.[44] Dr. Martin Luther King, Jr. was an idealist

---

[43] Wikipedia. (2018, November 30). "Leonardo DaVinci." Retrieved from https://en.wikipedia.org/wiki/Leonardo_da_Vinci

[44] Biography.com Editors. (2014, April 2). "Deepak Chopra Biography." Retrieved from https://www.biography.com/people/deepak-chopra-9542257

with an incredible, driving cause of equality.[45] He believed in the power of the collective to ignite change. Finally, Oprah Winfrey is a curator for those needing to share their stories, knowledge, and insights to help people live their best lives. She's done this through her television platform as well as her magazine.[46]

The types of roles those influencers have played in our society are possible for you to embody in your work as well, on whatever scale you choose. We'll cover each one in greater detail as we move through the chapter so that you can familiarize yourself with the ones you most resonate with and can potentially utilize to fulfill your unique purpose. You may ultimately decide that rather than choosing only one, you want to mix it up and become a little bit of several of them. Nothing is set in stone here. This is solely a guide to make it easier for you to assume your potential in the world and clarify the role you'll play in creating change.

The only thing that's necessary for you to do here is to take time to sit with each one of these roles and think about whether they resonate with you. See how each one feels to you as you consider yourself in these roles. Do

[45] Biography.com Editors. (2014, April 2). "Dr. Martin Luther King Jr. Biography." Retrieved from https://www.biography.com/people/martin-luther-king-jr-9365086
[46] Biography.com Editors. (2014, April 2). "Oprah Winfrey Biography." Retrieved from https://www.biography.com/people/oprah-winfrey-9534419

they make you feel expansive or closed off? Is there one that makes you feel nervous or scared to even think about? Are there any that make you excited to get started and do the work? Pay attention to your emotions and how your body responds as you read through them. That will give you much more insight into which ones are right for you than constant planning ever will. Let's dive in.

———————————

The innovator archetype is one that may come very naturally to you as a multi-passionate person. In fact, you may already be acting as an innovator every single day and just not realize it. As you put together your knowledge and experiences in a variety of different fields, you are creating new ideas. Being an innovator could literally mean that you're putting those ideas to use by inventing something brand new, or it could be that you're thinking about a new approach to doing things. It doesn't have to be on a massive scale like inventing an airplane. The smallest things can make the biggest impact on people's lives.

By combining your own interests and seeing where there may be intersections, you can spark change by connecting the dots. It's as if you're an engineer designing a bridge across knowledge areas so that people can use the best services or systems on either side and end up with a better result. Maybe you're plugging a hole on a leaking dam in a specific field with a patch from a different area of expertise. That patch may have never existed before because no one saw the connection between those two fields. It could be that you're an architect of sorts, and you lay a foundation for your tribe in one subject, but you teach them to grow with another.

The possibilities are endless when you're an innovator because there's always room to see things differently and make connections. We need innovators doing work like this in our society. Many times industries get stuck on what they've always done, but it takes someone with a different perspective to see the possibilities. In our previous example of Steve Jobs, we noted how he drew upon multiple areas of interest when he was building Apple into what it is now. He studied calligraphy, Buddhism, design, technology, and so much more. Because of that, he was able to piece together a new vision for what computers could be used for and how they could be intertwined into people's lives.[47]

Another example is Blake Mycoskie, the founder of Toms Shoes.[48] Mycoskie is an innovator in the way that he merged business with social impact to not only increase the bottom line of a company but to also make the world better. His goal was to make business about more than just consumerism. Mycoskie's vision went beyond

---

[47] Issacson, Walter. 2011. *Steve Jobs*. New York, New York: Simon & Schuster.

[48] Toms.com, LLC. (2018). "Blake Mycoskie." Retrieved from https://www.toms.com/blakes-bio

the typical idea of a non-profit in that he actually wanted the business to be profit-generating while still being socially responsible. Thus, his one-for-one method of how one purchased product would generate one product given away to someone in need was born. His forward-thinking is now part of a larger movement called social entrepreneurship where people around the world are choosing to do business in a more socially responsible manner that gives back to the world in some way.[49]

You may think that being an innovator is a pretty hefty task. If you look at it in terms of what's driving you, though, you can see that the choice may already be made for you. It's intrinsic to the way you see the world and is already within you. Can you see the gaps in knowledge that others can't see? Have you already identified ways by which people could be doing things better? You may have a vision for something that's years ahead of your colleagues, and that's nothing to be nervous about! As an innovator, you have an incredible gift of being a problem-solver and seeing beyond what's right in front of you.

Remember those three-dimensional pictures that would often be sold in wall art stores in local malls? They were the ones where the pattern looked all jumbled up. Yet, if

---

[49] Lumen Learning. (2018). "Case Study: Social Entrepreneurship at Tom's Shoes." Retrieved from https://courses.lumenlearning.com/ivytech-introbusiness/chapter/case-study-social-entrepreneurship-at-toms-shoes/

you stared at one of them for long enough, you could see something pop out of the pattern. It may have been a flower, a boat, or even a person. At first you didn't realize it was there, but once you changed your perspective a bit and looked closer, you could see it. That's what it's like to be an innovator. You have a perspective unlike anyone else. When you use it to ask questions, go deeper, and connect the dots, you have the incredible potential to solve problems and fill gaps to allow individuals, industries, or even society to grow leaps and bounds.

If you choose to play the innovator role as a change-maker, you need to be able to make those connections and bring them to light. You'll be the best-qualified person to do the job with your unique skills and experience, but confidence in your abilities will be an important part of your success. Recognize that not everyone will be able to see or accept the concepts you come up with, and that may in large part be due to people's natural resistance to change. Use your judgment about the best ways to present your work but also be diligent in getting your message across repeatedly for the biggest impact.

If you're feeling apprehensive about the idea of being an innovator, that's okay. It's best to trust your gut. On one hand, if you've got butterflies in your stomach thinking about it, then you may just be excited yet nervous about the potential of it. You could take that as a sign that your gut is leading you to it in order to challenge you. However, it may be telling you that while you do like combining various interests together, being an innovator may not be the best role for you to play. That's perfectly fine, too. There are plenty more ways for you to be of service in the world, and this one is just the beginning. Trusting your gut on this will always steer you in the right direction. As I've said before, you've been given the exact gifts and expertise you're supposed to have to do the work you're meant to do. Believe that your role will unfold to you exactly as it's supposed to, and just do your best to listen to what's inside of you along the way.

Now, that being said, if you do believe that you were meant to be an innovator, then stir yourself to action. The world needs people like you to create progress. Chances are that if you feel like you've got something you need to investigate, test out, or connect, then you're probably onto something that deserves further attention. Let that fuel your work and guide your decisions everyday. Set yourself up right from the beginning by honing in on your idea of success and what it would look like if you spread your core message through innovation. Use that vision to get yourself out of "idea mode" and put together the exact steps to get you moving forward. You don't want to leave the people who need you most waiting when you're fully capable of delivering a solution to them now.

Putting this into practice even further, you can look specifically at the fields you're familiar with that revolve around your core message. Make a list of the gaps or weaknesses you see in each one. How can you address those gaps with the additional knowledge or expertise that you have? Brainstorm any solutions you might have and see if any particular ones fit into your vision for spreading your message. Perhaps you've come up with a better way for busy parents to spend quality time with their kids. There may be a way of presenting this to fit in nicely with your idea of success. It could be writing a book series about it so that you can work from home and still reach your audience. It could be that you teach workshops so that you can travel nationwide and meet people in person to connect. You get to choose how you present your message in the world and address the problems you're solving, so be mindful of your idea of success from the get-go.

The other component of being an innovator is to collaborate as much as possible. Talk with people in multiple fields. Partner with others in ways that not only spread your message but also help you shift your own perspective. Research how people solve the same issues in various fields and how they differ. Test out many possibilities and use beta groups. The most helpful innovations can actually come from problem-solving as a collective rather than in a vacuum. Even though you may think you have a solution that works, sometimes it's really best to put your head together with others and collaborate to make it even better.

Once you've done the visualizing and testing, then you've got to implement. It'll be up to you to choose how best to present your ideas, but putting them out there in the world is critical. You'll never know how your concepts and ideas can truly serve others until you're brave enough to take a chance on them. Feedback is a necessity for engendering progress. Even negative reviews can be worthwhile learning points. They'll help you see how people do things in real life rather than solely in your mind or how small adjustments can make a world of difference.

When I was in architecture school, we would hold design reviews of our projects at least twice per semester. People would stay up all night for several nights in a row leading up to the big reviews. They would work on their building design drawings and models painstakingly to get them prepped to go before a panel of professors who judged the feasibility of the work as well as the conceptual designs. It was a brutal process at times where I saw a number of students get verbally torn apart over their work. There were also instances where professors would literally tear apart the student's models in order to make a point and show them what needed to be changed. Many times it was incredibly demoralizing not to mention a bit humiliating, but you had to have a strong backbone to make it through the program and through a career in design.

I realized after having a few of my own bad reviews, including one that had me in the bathroom crying in the end, that I had to take myself out of the equation in order to be a better problem-solver. It wasn't about me or the work that I wanted to do at all. Instead, it was about how the work was able to serve the greater good, which in that case was the user of the building we were creating. It was about getting feedback so that the people who needed it most would benefit from it, not protect my own ego as the designer. Yes, I was putting my heart into the work to make it the best it could be. Once I put it out into the world, though, I had to learn to let it be whatever it needed to be. Detaching myself from the outcome was probably one of the best lessons I learned from architecture school. It enabled me to keep getting back on the horse as a diligent problem-solver rather than being wrapped up in how my idea should be the best and last solution.

Be mindful of how innovation goes hand in hand with service. Just because you're the innovator, it doesn't mean that people will take everything you say as gospel. The audience you're trying to serve gets the last word. They're the ones who'll ultimately decide if your solution works for them and if they're ready to implement it. While it's great to be adamant about your approach, it's also wise to understand that feedback is the best friend to constant improvement. If you're willing to set aside your own ego and intentions to make room for the true needs of your audience, then you can do great things as an innovator.

Usually we think of an artist as someone who is constantly creating thought-provoking work in a certain
medium. As the entrepreneurial role of a creator, you
expressively create a body of work based on your core
message. It's about doing soulful work that comes out in
various forms and draws from your many passions.
Then, as you present the work to your followers, the
intention is to really contemplate it or feel a deeper
connection to it somehow. Being a creator always comes
from the heart, and you must truly follow what inspires
you to fill this role in society.

The creator role goes really well with building a personal brand and being quite prolific in what you do. You
have the ability to span a variety of different mediums
with all the pieces of your work and bridge them all
together under one umbrella of your brand. It gives you
the distinction of your core message, while at the same
time allowing you to freely express yourself as you
choose. Of all the potential roles for you to play as a
multi-passionate entrepreneur, this one has the most
open-ended opportunity for self-expression of them all.

However, don't think the role of a creator is only tailored
to the arts. You could most certainly have your own take
on this in fields such as science, sociology, or even technology. There's always room to be expressive and do
something outside of the box to spark inspiration and
thought in others. It's all in what you make of your
circumstances, and you'll need to use some ingenuity at

times to figure out the best way to be expressive and get your message across. If you believe yourself to be a creator, though, then there's no better way to express yourself than by trusting your inner compass to guide your work.

Now, I am going to give you a couple examples here of those in art-centric fields, but only for the purpose of them being easy to set your frame of reference. That way you'll have a couple popular examples that can be at the top of your mind when you're working towards your own role as a creator. It's always good to see the possible and then take it even further. So once you understand the concept here, you can apply this role to creators in multiple fields including some in your own.

First, Justin Timberlake comes to mind when I think of a modern-age creator.[50] Timberlake is a talented celebrity known widely throughout the world, and his body of work is in the performing arts as a singer, dancer, actor, and producer. He got his start on several TV shows at a young age and then became known for being a lead singer in the pop music group, N'Sync. Now, he has a massive personal brand based around being a "triple

---

[50] Biography.com Editors. (2014, April 1). "Justin Timberlake Biography." Retrieved by https://www.biography.com/ people/justin-timberlake-201200

threat" in multiple genres.[51] As an example of what it means to be a creator, you can see that he has a very broad portfolio centered around his main focus of performing.

A prolific performing artist from a previous generation was Liza Minnelli.[52] As a singer, dancer, and actress, she expressed herself through the stage. Minnelli grew up in a performing family, and went into the business at an incredibly young age. Getting to share her talents with others became a very fruitful, lifelong career for her and she moved from movies to television and also Broadway.[53] Minnelli is another example of how sharing your talents across multiple genres can be a powerful way to connect with the people who need you the most.

The last widely known person I want to recognize here is Tina Fey, who is known for her comedy.[54] Fey began as a working comedian and was in the popular Second City comedy group in Chicago. She won acclaim on the tele-

[51] Biography.com Editors. (2014, April 1). "Justin Timberlake Biography." Retrieved by https://www.biography.com/people/justin-timberlake-201200

[52] Biography.com Editors. (2014, April 2). "Liza Minnelli Biography." Retrieved from https://www.biography.com/people/liza-minnelli-9409583

[53] Biography.com Editors. (2014, April 2). "Liza Minnelli Biography." Retrieved from https://www.biography.com/people/liza-minnelli-9409583

[54] Fey, Tina. (2014, April 2). "Tina Fey Biography." Retrieved from https://www.biography.com/people/tina-fey-365284

vision series *Saturday Night Live*, went on to become an actress in several movies, and is now a published author. Fey advocates for strong women in her work while always adding humor and levity to her roles as well. She has developed a bit of a cult following for her humor and what she brings to each project.[55] Looking at Tina Fey's success as a creator, you can see that people are drawn to her personality and how she presents herself in the world. This is her form of expression, and it radiates from her in everything she does.

There are so many different ways you can assume the role of a creator. It may be through the performing arts as in these examples. It could be through opening a few different product-based businesses. Maybe you'd like to be a photographer that publishes coffee table photography books, holds art gallery shows, and sells stock photos. You could be a software designer who creates an iPhone app in one field, provides background systems for entrepreneurs to run their businesses, and sells website templates through an online store. What makes each of these people a creator is the fact that they've each chosen to span their unifying message across a broad body of work.

Your body of work, or portfolio, includes everything you create, publish, offer, or develop. It's the sum of all the things you do, and each one individually is representa-

[55] Fey, Tina. (2014, April 2). "Tina Fey Biography." Retrieved from https://www.biography.com/people/tina-fey-365284

tive of the whole. Usually, that's by connecting with your message. You'll have stand alone pieces of work that you've done with any number of your interests and talents. Those will allow you to offer solutions to specific problems or address specific needs in the marketplace. They will individually help you connect with your ideal customers as you hone in on the key ways that you understand them and what they're going through. Yet, overall, when someone sees your entire body of work, it'll be the entirety of your messaging. That is, it's the curated introduction to what you stand for, and it gives people the opportunity to dive deeper into the components as suited.

In order to be successful at this, you must be able to see the big picture of how your core message serves the world and then also see how the pieces work to support it. Think of it this way. If you were applying to art school, you would need to submit a portfolio of your work to the admissions board to be considered. In it, you'd probably need to include work from not only your main area of concentration but also from a few other interest areas that compliment that main one. Doing this shows your creative capability and broad range as an artist as well as someone willing to use multiple forms of expression to drive a conversation or movement. The same is true when you're building your brand's body of work. You not only should show work from one select field but also branch out and create other pieces in tangential subjects. This way, you'll be able to drive home your message through multiple mediums to make the most impact.

Putting this into practice, if it feels like this role suits you, then you should take time to consider the big picture of where you ultimately want to be in your career—the end goal. As you complete a variety of projects, they may have different paths associated with them traditionally. A photography path could be aimed at getting magazine work. A writing path could be aimed at being on the bestseller lists. If you're combining multiple types of work into one brand, you've got to be very clear about how you want them to converge in the end. That could include anything from positioning you as a multifaceted expert in your messaging all the way to landing you a deal with a major company you'd love to represent publicly. So, visualize the idea of what success means to you, and ensure that the work you include in your portfolio makes sense for getting you to that picture in your mind.

Action Exercise:

We always think about success in terms of money or status, but it can be so different for each and every one of us. As multi-passionate entrepreneurs, we're not on the typical path that everyone else is on, which is a good thing! The standard idea of building a business based on putting your head down for years and years and focusing on doing one thing well, while instilling a strong work ethic, is actually an antiquated idea that no longer serves many of us well. It tells us that things have to be hard to be fruitful. It reiterates that you can only be good at something if it's the only thing you ever focus on, or that your business won't grow if people see you doing anything but the one thing they expect of you.

Nowadays, as we discussed at the beginning of the book, we're living in a time where people refuse to settle for careers that are unfulfilling or put them in a box. That especially includes those of us that have so much to give in terms of our strengths and interests. That's why when you think about your definition of success, I want you to reconsider all the things that you've been taught. Dare to think differently, and be bold enough to think big. If you can visualize it, you can realize it.

Changing the way you approach your business starts with the way you want to approach your life. You create your own reality, so you must give yourself a leg up from the very beginning by being clear in your own mind. If you are clear about what success means in your own life and also the achievement or change you hope for in others, then you've got a direction. That's a goal or future reality to shoot for, and everything else can fall into place from there.

In order to do this, recognize that little steps will add up to the big accomplishment you hope to eventually achieve. You might have to do this by working on lots of different projects or by creating many offers to achieve your own vision of success. Ultimately, the progression of how you'll get there will start with your big vision of success.

So in this exercise, that's exactly where you're going to start. Give yourself a quiet space to sit for at least ten minutes. Calm your mind and ensure nothing is worrying you or stressing you out at the moment. Allow yourself to think of something comforting that makes you happy in order to get your mind working in the direction of positive thinking. Tell yourself that you are meant to be happy and fulfilled. You are meant to achieve your dreams, and if you let it, the universe will align to what's best for you so that you may let what's inside of you shine.

When you're ready to begin thinking about your future vision, let your mind go to where you're happiest. Think about the things you would be doing as your best and happiest self. Does that include taking photos, writing, playing sports, raising a family, or something else? Picture yourself doing those specific things and allow yourself to lean into how it actually feels to be in those moments.

Ask yourself what your best life looks like. What would it be like if everything aligned so that you could achieve exactly what you wanted? How would your business and personal life look? Where would you be working? Who would you be serving or helping? How would you be presenting it in the world? The more clear you can be on the specifics of what you want, the better.

To follow this up, take another look at the feelings and emotions you want to feel in that moment when everything is aligned for you. This is the complementary part of visualizing in which you also feel the emotion as if you already have those things and have achieved the success you want. Sit with those emotions and recognize what they've come as a result of in your life. Try to pinpoint at least two or three feelings that you'd like to tie to your vision of success in this way, and be specific about the ways that you intend to create those feelings in your life.

Close your thoughts in this session by acknowledging your inner compass, guiding you to become the person you're meant to be. Be grateful for the gifts and talents that you have to share and the ability to go on this journey in sharing them with the world. As one last reminder, tell yourself that continuing to clarify your vision of success will allow you to more fully realize your purpose.

This exercise should help you greatly in figuring out exactly where you want to go and how to do the work you're meant to do in the world. Also, by being clear about the intentions you have, the feeling you want to create, and the way your work looks in the world, you'll be able to give yourself that same vision in your head every time the going gets tough and you need something to focus on to get you through it. Because you'll know exactly what you're working toward and why that matters to you so much.

In addition, you'll have a much better understanding of what it takes to get there. Remember, you need to know where you're going before you can build the road to get you there. Unless you're still discovering how your passions fit together and how you can be of value to people, there's really no point in heading down a path without having a picture in your head of exactly where you want to go. You're most likely not going to go on a road trip across the country without some idea of where you'll end up. You might if you had all the time in the world and were exploring for fun. Of course, exploration is absolutely fine. You should do that in the beginning stages of your business anyway. However, just know, that if you're serious about this entrepreneurship thing, your big vision for what success means to you can be the thing that keeps you on track, no matter what comes your way.

Keep that picture in your head of the specific things you're striving for and tell yourself that it's a done deal. It's going to happen. You don't have to stress or worry about it because you're on your way, and the universe will align to support you in getting there. Just sink into the relief that you don't have to worry anymore because that vision will become a reality.

Now that you've done the exercise to identify your idea of success, this is your chance to solidify that into your big why. Get to the heart of that vision you have to determine what the driving force is behind it all. Is it so that you can have a location-independent life while making an impact on people around the world? Is it so that you can work with a small team of local people who are inspired to create change? Is it so that you have more time for your family but can still grow a million dollar company?

Your vision of success is dictated by your big why, so you just need to see the underlying reasoning behind your vision. Then, it's your job to keep that vision and big why in your head while you do the work, because it won't all just miraculously happen. You have to take the steps to get yourself there and then trust that it will unfold in time.

That's the hard part. That's where you need that vision and big why to carry you through the hard times where you don't quite see things aligning the way you want them to. That's when you still need to believe that it will all work out. Most importantly, that's when you need to pick yourself up, dust yourself off, and say, "How can I keep myself on track toward my goal?"

Your big why will be the thing that carries you through everything if you make it so clear that there's no denying exactly what you want so you can always find a way to keep working toward it. Let it drive you. Let it push you past the hard times and give you the strength you need to keep going. If you need to create a vision board, do it. If you need to write out your big why on a sticky note and post it to your computer screen, do it. If you need to have it as the screensaver on your phone so you can see it every morning right when you wake up, then do it. Your big vision is the key to everything. Once again, you have to be clear enough to identify exactly what you want and willing to let go of the stress of how you're going to get there.

Your inner compass will guide you if you allow yourself to let go enough. However, I'm a firm believer that a foundation of planning is well worth the time spent to do it. Thus, I'm going to give you a framework for how to create a plan for yourself starting with your vision for success and your big why and working backwards. The intention of this is to make you feel comfortable enough to step out and take action. You can always change course later if you feel your gut taking over and telling you that something's not quite right. Initially, though, your plan will serve as your roadmap. You may have forks in the road or end up having to take a road less traveled, but at least you'll be able to follow a course of action to get you headed in the direction you want to go.

To do this, sit with the thought of your big vision for success and the idea of why you're doing it all in the first place. Identify the pieces of that vision that gave you the feelings you were after. If you wanted to feel fulfilled, was it because you had plenty of family time? If you wanted to feel accomplished, was it because you became a bestselling author? Make a list of the specific components that are a part of your vision. Detail them out so that you can see individual pieces of the puzzle. One may be that you are an inspiring coach while another is that you are a volunteer in your community. Your list may be as little as three or four things or as long as ten. It's up to you to define the components that make up your vision and fall under your big why.

Starting with an endpoint in mind and then detailing out the specifics of getting there is something that every good designer and project manager knows how to do. As someone with a background in both, I can tell you that your concept is everything. You base your entire design and your entire project around the concept or the vision. Then, you put the pieces together for the details, but it always starts with the concept design. This vision is your concept design. In project management, once you know the end goal, you gather information, put together the critical steps you need to take in order to achieve it, and the rest falls in line from there. That's exactly what I want you to do as well.

Now that you've made a list of the individual components that make up your vision, here's where you'll put together the critical steps to get you there. You want to look at each component separately to lay out the path that makes sense for each one. That way you won't be overextending yourself as you go to work on each project you want to accomplish. I know, you're saying that you don't want to get bored with doing one thing at a time. Don't get bogged down with the details of how you'll get everything accomplished right now. Just focus on defining each project path so that you have your roadmap for what you want. You can always adjust your timeline for specific endeavors according to what suits you best and what you're feeling inspired to work on at the time.

Getting back to laying out your steps, take one of the things that you'd like to achieve such as being a published author. On the same page where you've been making your list, write this specific objective out in its own section. Underneath it, begin to list out all of the steps you know of currently to get you to that end goal. For instance, you know you need to brainstorm book ideas, outline your book, write the rough draft, have it edited, and then market the book when it comes out. Those are the critical steps to get you to your end point. The more you research about the process, the more you'll be able to fill in the details and the specific tasks. For now, though, you have an understanding of the milestones that will get you closer to achieving that one piece of your overall vision of success.

You can go through each component of your big vision and repeat this process to define the milestone steps of each one. When you've done them all, it may seem a bit daunting to look at your entire page and see how much you've actually got to do! Rest assured, that it's all totally surmountable! You've already done a considerable bit of work to get started by outlining the steps you need to take to get there. Now, you just need to make some decisions about what you'd like to focus on first in order to build up to your overall vision.

These exercises should serve as confidence boosters for you to know that you can figure out exactly how to get to where you want to be. All it takes is the ability to work backward. There's no secret sauce to becoming successful other than being diligent, constructing a foundational plan, and letting your inner compass guide you to what's right for you. You can achieve every component of your big vision if you allow yourself some grace in how and when you get there. So, stop worrying about where you should be by now or what everyone else says you should be doing. Just keep your eye on your roadmap to get to where you want to be. The purposeful work will follow from there.

This takes us to the third role of a multi-passionate entrepreneur: the thought leader. In this particular role, you present a new perspective or way of looking at something and lead a movement toward that new paradigm. This may seem like a bit of a modern position to take, so let's identify what preconceived notions you may have about it first. Do you have a certain idea already in your mind of what type of people are thought leaders? Do you think they need to always be out in the public eye giving speeches and leading the charge? You might think it has to be someone who is open about their life and all they do like a politician running for election. On the other hand, maybe you view thought leaders to be on a whole other level from normal people, as if that role is for those garnering high acclaim, possibly beyond anything you've considered achieving for yourself.

In today's society, however, you can be a thought leader at every level, on a massive, world-wide scale like Dalai Lama, on a national scale like former President Barack Obama, or even in your state or local community or organization. All it means is that you have an idea for how things should be different, and you're ready to lead the charge to make the change. It means being ready to step up and support your ideas with your strengths and experience and have the guts to take the lead where others will follow. In some cases, this could mean that you need to be more visible publicly in order to get your message across and draw attention to your ideas. However, that's not a complete requirement. You could easily run smaller campaigns or be known in a small circle of necessary individuals that will help you make the changes you desire. Remember, nothing is set in stone, and these roles that I'm presenting for your consideration are only guides to give you a little more clarity.

Now, as far as whether people in thought leader roles are considered on another level of acclaim, that is a completely subjective viewpoint. I will tell you, though, that it is possible for you as a multi-passionate person to be a thought leader at any level. It is not something that you should view as unattainable by any means. As you piece together your core message, you may very well find that being a thought leader has been in you all along, and that this truly is the right role for you to play in being a change-maker. If it feels right, get comfortable with the idea that you were meant to lead with the exact combination of skills and talents that you have, and that it's now time to embrace a more active role.

To help you in seeing what's possible, I'll once again give you some examples. First, we'll look at the author, speaker, and digital age marketing and business guru, Seth Godin.[56] He founded the online company Squidoo.com for sharing information and ideas, and he is now known as a business leader in the information age. Godin wrote several books including *Purple Cow* and *Tribes*, where he's talked about the power of standing out in the marketplace and being able to grow a loyal following or tribe.[57] Many entrepreneurs and business

---

[56] Editors, TheFamousPeople.com. (2017, January 5). "Seth Godin Biography." Retrieved from https://www.thefamouspeople.com/profiles/seth-godin-2833.php
[57] Editors, TheFamousPeople.com. (2017, January 5). "Seth Godin Biography." Retrieved from https://www.thefamouspeople.com/profiles/seth-godin-2833.php

people look to Godin for guidance on how to stand out in crowded industries and market based on their uniqueness. His concept of tribes has also spread like wildfire across entrepreneurial circles with those eager to grow their personal brands and online businesses.

What about the author, Simon Sinek, who has spread the thought-provoking work from his book, *Start With Why?*, Sinek started in the business world, spent time figuring out why he was doing the things he did to be successful, and realized that he needed to understand the reasoning behind it all.[58] His TedTalk speech along the same lines as the book launched him into thought leader territory with his passionate approach to the way everyone should approach their work.[59] Sinek has been incredibly impactful in business and entrepreneurial circles as he advocates for understanding the bigger picture behind your actions to be more fulfilled in life and work. His work continues to spread even further as he now discusses leadership and what it takes to be a leader at any level. Looking at his approach to being a thought leader, you can see Sinek shares his message primary through books and speaking platforms, but his message has spread incredibly from there.

---

[58] Van Vliet, V. (2014). *Simon Sinek*. Retrieved from https://www.toolshero.com/toolsheroes/simon-sinek/
[59] TED Conferences, LLC. (2018). "Simon Sinek, Leadership Expert." Retrieved from https://www.ted.com/speakers/simon_sinek

As one more example in this category, we can look at Tony Robbins. It's hard to find someone in the Western world who doesn't know of Tony Robbins as a motivational speaker. He's built a massive business as an author of several books, speaker to thousands, and coach on leadership.[60] The website, Inc.com, calls him the man that modernized the idea of a thought leader because he was one of the very first to build a platform for his message in this way. Through his work, Robbins focuses on helping people improve their lives through the power of decision-making, creating change, and developing mastery within yourself and key areas of your life. He has guided millions on their self-development journeys and continues to do so.[61] The power of his role as a thought leader is in the confidence he carries in himself and his message across many communication platforms.

As you can see, there are some pretty powerful examples of thought leaders, and the ones I've discussed have been on a fairly large scale. Being the frontrunner for a certain way of thinking can be scary as you have a big responsibility to lead people, but it can also be incredibly fulfilling. You get to show the world a necessary view-

---

[60] Eades, John. (2017, May 24). "10 Thought Leaders You Should Be Following to be More Successful." Retrieved from https://www.inc.com/john-eades/10-thought-leaders-you-should-be-following-to-be-more-successful.html
[61] Eades, John. (2017, May 24). "10 Thought Leaders You Should Be Following to be More Successful." Retrieved from https://www.inc.com/john-eades/10-thought-leaders-you-should-be-following-to-be-more-successful.html

point that can serve them immensely. You get to combine your years of experience, struggles, and insights to reveal a better way of doing things. Being the one that stirs up new ideas means ultimately, though, that you are in the lead. You have to be strong enough to accept that there will be criticism and resistance to change but at the same time realize that your message needs to be heard above all else.

Thus, thought leadership is not for the faint of heart. If you feel an inclination toward being a thought leader, then make sure you find a way to keep yourself going strong both mentally and emotionally as you lead the way. You've got to take care of yourself in order to take care of others, and in this role, it's especially true. As you build your business, be diligent to safeguard your time and energy as best you can and set priorities for everything you do. This will ensure that you have the most energy to devote to your audience in the most impactful ways.

In order to put this role into practice as you build, make sure you have your big, core overarching message that you've defined. The thing that's driving everything you do will quite likely go hand in hand with how you become a thought leader and establish yourself. So, sort that out with exactly how your ideas will help people solve problems. Also, think about your vision of success here as well. What will it look and feel like when you successfully get your message across in the world? What platform do you want to use to get that message across?

How do you want to help people put it into practice in their lives? When you have a clear picture of this, you can piece together what you should work on to get you there. It may be that you start a blog first. Then, you may choose to host webinars on specific topics or apply to speak at local organizations. Start with your idea of success, choose your platform, and identify the work that sounds most fulfilling to you. That will all help you get closer to spreading your message in the way that makes the most sense for you.

This next role is one I'm going to argue feels like the biggest amount of responsibility. It probably makes sense for you if you're one that holds a cause near and dear to your heart or if you've got something that you hold as a key belief at your very core. When you find yourself doing work regularly toward that one key belief in a variety of different ways, then you most likely are an idealist. The role of idealists is to bring people together over a chosen cause. They advocate for change in many different ways but always come back to the driving message related to their cause and how they can promote it in the world to bring about a shift.

One of the people that immediately comes to mind for me as an idealist is Gloria Steinem, women's advocate and founder of Ms magazine.[62] As a writer primarily, Steinem first championed her cause for women and equality as a freelancer. She then went on to write articles and books along with starting her magazine. She is a lecturer and activist with a long history of being an advocate for the cause she believes in so strongly, and this cause of women's equality has become her life's work. It's the thing she's best known for...not being a writer or the founder of the magazine, but overall as a woman who furthered the women's equality movement in the public domain and encouraged others to strive for equality as well.[63] That's a powerful legacy to leave when you're defined by a message much bigger than you are, and the work you've done toward that end has moved masses.

Another idealist who is not only an advocate for social change but for political and governmental change as well is Michael Moore.[64] Moore is a documentary filmmaker, author, and activist known for his judgmental critiques of capitalism, weapons ownership, and the war in Iraq. His work has spanned many mediums and has

---

[62] History.com Editors. (2009, December 16). "Gloria Steinem." Retrieved from https://www.history.com/topics/womens-history/gloria-steinem

[63] History.com Editors. (2009, December 16). "Gloria Steinem." Retrieved from https://www.history.com/topics/womens-history/gloria-steinem

[64] IMBD.com. (2018). "Michael Moore Biography." Retrieved from https://www.imdb.com/name/nm0601619/bio

won awards including an Academy Award. Moore definitely has a strong following of supporters who back his idealism and stance on many issues. If you look at his career as a means to present his unifying theme of transparency in social issues, you can see that each piece of his work is clearly representative of that in many different ways. He's brought to light several important issues in his films including Bowling for Columbine and Fahrenheit 9/11.[65] His books have called out many political administrations, and he's always addressing topics that he believes the American population should be concerned with.[66]

If you've considered yourself to be an idealist as you read through these examples, then you're most definitely in good company among many who have put their work ahead of themselves to make strides for the greater good. Looking at the journey of being an idealist, you'll have to be bold enough to use your voice and become tough enough to weather the ups and downs of how society takes your message. Conviction is the biggest thing you've got on your side, though, along with your experiences and background, so you'll have to use them purposefully. The best way to put this into practice is through the use of storytelling to motivate your tribe of followers. You must make strong emotional connections

[65] IMBD.com. (2018). "Michael Moore Biography." Retrieved from https://www.imdb.com/name/nm0601619/bio
[66] IMBD.com. (2018). "Michael Moore Biography." Retrieved from https://www.imdb.com/name/nm0601619/bio

built on common ground and common understanding. Show people that you know what troubles them, where they're coming from, and how they feel. We'll discuss storytelling a bit more in the coming chapter, but it's important to note that this is a highly valuable tool for idealists wanting to lead a movement and connect with others over a common belief.

For our final role, this is the one that's based around facilitating. The role of the curator is done by making the space to bring things or people together in new and different ways. It could be through facilitating an open discussion. It could be through planning an event like a conference. Just think about it like you would a curator for a museum. Curators carefully select the work that will be in each of the exhibits in order to have a well-balanced complete display that accomplishes their intention. As a curating entrepreneur, it would be your job to assemble parts into a whole based on your passions and expertise. You would use your unique perspective on the world to compile the best and most useful resources you can around your chosen topic.

Many people are turning to virtual summits currently as a way of doing this in the digital, information age. They bring together a group of anywhere from ten to thirty influencers and guest speakers focused on a specific topic and facilitate the online conference as a means to walk attendees through the know-how on a subject. It's a way to gather a wealth of knowledge together and in doing so also position yourself as an expert in the subject matter that you're facilitating. Curators can also be found all over social media. Bloggers, coaches, and small business owners in every field are setting up their social profiles and curating content to suit their audiences. You're most likely in this category as well as someone who has already started or about to start your own business. Social media is a critical component of your strategy and having the ability to curate the right content for your audience is imperative.

But on a larger scale as a curator at your core, you've got to approach your business endeavors with the intention of contribution and building community. Those are the two guiding principles here that will allow you to be a more successful curator. In saying that, I want to introduce two examples of successful curators today. The first is Chase Jarvis, the photographer and creative behind the business, Creative Live.[67] As a constant creative that thrives on inspiration and expression, Jarvis built a space where people could take courses and trainings on a variety of different creative endeavors including everything from product photography to candle-making. Creative Live now has an online platform as well as

---

[67] Schwabel, Dan. (2017, January 24). "Chase Jarvis: How He Became The Photographer Everyone Wants To Work With." Retrieved from https://www.forbes.com/sites/danschawbel/2014/01/27/chase-jarvis-how-he-became-the-photographer-everyone-wants-to-work-with/#60661139118b

having two US West Coast based offices. In each space, business owners, artists, and experts give presentations and share their knowledge on a daily basis so that others can learn to use their gifts for further self-expression and possibly even to grow a business.[68] The incredible platform has given creative knowledge a means to be consolidated on a large scale and reach people all over the world.

Grace Bonney, the founder of the popular website Design Sponge, is another example of how to build a business around being a curator.[69] She is an author and host of in-person events as well as a radio show. Bonney started as a design column writer and magazine editor and build her online platform to bring the design community down to meet people where they are in their lives with both their homes and businesses. She brings entrepreneurs and creatives together in the space she has created through blog interviews, designer highlights, and the lifestyle centric information she aggregates on her blog platform. You can see that her successful online platform is about gathering ideas around a common theme of design inspiration and that the simple act of

---

[68] Creative Live, Inc. (2018). "In Studio." Retrieved from https://www.creativelive.com/in-studio
[69] Design Sponge, LLC. (2018). "About." Retrieved from https://www.designsponge.com/about

meeting people where they are with this topic has res-
onated profoundly with her audience.[70]

As a curator, you have the ability to create any platform
to bring information and people together. If you resonate
with being a curator, the biggest steps you can take are
to acknowledge the arena in which you want to curate
information--most likely around your core driving message. Then, you need to identify the best platform on
which for you to do it. Whether that's a blog, podcast,
workshop, or a combination of platforms, you get to
choose which way suits your gifts and talents best and
which would be best received by your audience. Then,
start making connections with people who can contribute information and provide value around your
message. Remember, facilitating the discussion or the
information is what your role should be here, so you
don't need to do it all. You only have to provide the
means for it all to come together. Get out and network to
build relationships. Seek out people with complementary ideas and gifts to share who may work well with
others in your space. Build a community of engagement
and participation within the space or platform you create. That is how you grow a following and a business
using the power of being a curator.

---

[70] Design Sponge, LLC. (2018). "About." Retrieved from
https://www.designsponge.com/about

I've shown you five roles that you could choose to follow as a multi-passionate entrepreneur to get your message across. If only one stands out to you then go with that. However, in all likelihood, you're going to want to choose at least two of those to implement for your brand. Combining two or three ways to position yourself and build your platforms is a completely viable option and one where you'll be able to stand out even more in your approach in the marketplace. Just be sure to pinpoint what you're going for early on to give you some direction, and then you can build your business framework around the roles you want to play.

With any of these roles, you've got to have the courage to put yourself out there in creating new ideas. These are all about utilizing your many unique talents and skills in a way that merges ideas and creates new perspectives for people. It's not solely about becoming an expert on one specific thing as it would be if you were choosing a niche. Rather, you're establishing yourself for what you stand for in life. You become the driver of the conversation out in the marketplace because of your belief and your unique perspective. That is what makes this a much more powerful alternative to the typical niche for multi-passionate people like you. Utilizing these roles with your core message allows you to wield your toolbox of gifts and talents to create your very own niche and not have to compete with anyone else in the process. Hopefully now, too, you're starting to realize how to piece together every single one of those tools in a more focused and intentional way.

Also realize that no matter which roles you choose, you can be a leader in your own right. You need to step up and own each position that you assume. If you feel yourself getting a bit hesitant about that, it's okay and completely normal. Just fall back on the importance of your message and the fact that people are waiting to hear from you. So as I've said before, you have to take yourself out of the equation and step into the spotlight for others that need you. It's no longer about you. It's about the message the world needs that only you can provide in your unique way. These entrepreneurial roles are just a means to help wrap your head around the best way to get your ideas across. They are your presentation method, and next you'll be coupling those with a framework for how to deliver your work most effectively.

Part Three

Realize Your Vision

Chapter Six

Building Your Business Framework

Now that your core message has been covered along with the role you want to play in presenting your message to the world, the next step is to establish the actual business model and branding for what you want. This will be the basic framework for your business so that you know how you plan to run it and create offers or products based around your interests. Think about this in terms of a construction project for a moment. Your core message is like the foundation of your building, and the role you play is the general type of building that you're creating, whether that be a house, store, skyscraper, or even a barn. On top of that strong foundation and knowing the purpose of your building, you need to have plans for the components that will go into your building. Will it have a garage, a parking lot, or a carport? Will it be a one-story ranch, a walk-up, or a multi-story apartment building? This is like your business model that gives you the mold to which you'll shape your business.

Some typical business models include those for franchises, multi-level marketing, freelance work, intellectual property sales, and even one-on-one coaching to name just a few. In the case of being a multi-passionate entrepreneur, I'm going to show you two effective ways to model your business around your many passions. Choose one that feels the most in line with your big vision for success and what you hope to achieve. You can always make adjustments as you go, but it's important to at least make some sort of choice in the beginning to get you moving. Keep in mind that you're never confined to your first decision. So, don't stress over this too much.

Do your best to use your intuition here to try to feel out what you know deep down works best for you. You can alter any of the framework pieces I give you to suit your own needs. As always, my goal is to give you a guide and show you a better way to put some parameters around all the things you do. Part of the problem with having so many different options to choose from when it comes to what you can do is that it leaves the decision-making so wide open. By choosing a framework, you actually give yourself more creative flexibility than you would without parameters because you're guiding your mind toward a direction. It's always easier to think of ideas given a few boundaries rather than with infinite possibilities.

However, don't disregard the importance of flexibility. When it comes to entrepreneurship, it is like a choose-your-own adventure book. You're the one that gets to decide the right path and which direction you'll turn. Start with a framework, let yourself feel it out, see how it works for you, and be ready to adjust. Changes are inevitable as you learn what will serve your audience best and how you best like to work. The critical piece of the puzzle is just that you decide to keep moving forward and taking action no matter what. You don't want to get stuck in planning mode or spinning your wheels on something that isn't getting you anywhere. If you get any signs from your gut telling you that what you're doing isn't working or that you're getting antsy to move on, it's perfectly fine to pivot.

This might be a good time to mention, though, that there is a certain amount of "stick-to-it-iveness" that you'll need in order to make your business venture a success. That's where paying attention to your inner clock comes up and making sure that you're giving yourself enough space to pursue what inspires you at any given time. The importance of doing projects will come in handy for you, and we'll discuss this in a later chapter. At this point, just realize that you will need to give each thing you're working on a fair amount of time to see if it sticks. If you decide it doesn't, then that's where you become flexible and shift your framework as needed.

Running a business as a multi-passionate person means
that you need to accommodate the constant pull of your
attention and need for changing up what you're working on. This is not something that others will greatly
understand and appreciate especially when many so-
called experts tout the imperativeness of niching down
to be great at one specific thing. Therefore, you've got to
look at your business from the standpoint of how it fuels
you as the creator. How is it going to give you the ability
to showcase your many gifts? How is it going to allow
you to tap into what inspires you at any given moment?
How is it going to give you the space you need to explore different areas of interest? These are the questions
you have to ask yourself before you go building your
business off a model that's built for someone with a
single focus.

This is what got me into trouble for so long when I was
trying to figure out exactly what business would be right
for me. I was constantly searching for the thing that I
was meant to do or that one business model that I could
build off of forever. I tried the service-based businesses
with event planning and logo design. I tried creating my
own products with invitation and party supply design. I
even tried blogging when we were overseas, and I was
cooking and traveling extensively. After all of that and
even more, I finally realized years later that I was never
going to get to that perfect business. It just didn't exist. I
will always be someone who works in many different

capacities and in many different disciplines, and that's okay.

Then how did I determine that there is a framework you can use as a multi-passionate entrepreneur? Well after I made that realization, I stopped looking for the one perfect business. I started looking instead at my own career progression and how it could all be merged. After taking countless entrepreneurship courses and training and pulling from my background in project management, I began to see that you could use a couple of basic business models to work to your advantage as a multi-passionate person. You could actually use them to make yourself stand out in the sea of all the other entrepreneurs in the marketplace because these models would allow you to be different. They would allow you to express your many passions fully and not hold you back in terms of the way you're meant to present your gifts to the world.

I made it a point to hash out these business models for myself and start implementing this process in my own career. Not only have I seen much more interest in what I'm doing in the world, but it's also given me the ability to focus on clear, intentional projects that are fulfilling and getting me closer to my own big vision of success. That's exactly what I want for you as well. I want you to feel excited that you get to wake up every single day and do the work that matters to you most, whatever that happens to be on any given day. I want you to feel fulfilled knowing that you're making a difference by combining your unique talents the way they were meant to be shared with the world. On top of all that, I want you to be successful as an entrepreneur who has the ability to shape your own career and brand into exactly what you want it to be.

That is my reasoning behind honing in on these two specific business models that I'm about to walk you through. Give yourself time to read through them a few times and allow the ideas behind them to sink in a bit. Just as you've done with the previous exercises in the book, listen to what your inner compass is telling you about each one and whether it suits you or not. Pay attention to the way your body feels when you think about them both and if there's that feeling of expansion or contraction. That will provide a huge insight into which path you should try first.

To start with, I want to give you a model that is roughly viewed as a traditional business approach that you've most likely been trying to make work already. For our intents as multi-passionates, we'll call this your experiential path. In this approach, you can focus on a primary passion or interest area, create a twist on it, and then turn it into a complete customer experience. How you do this is by focusing your efforts primarily on one centric discipline of yours first. I know that doesn't seem to make sense in the context of all we've been discussing, but stick with me. You want to be able to help people solve specific problems, and you may have one skill set that stands out in this respect above all else. That's where you're going to monopolize on that amazing skill you have and use it to cater to your audience primarily. In doing so, you are essentially using the typical idea of a business niche.

However, at the same time, you want to position yourself with a unique twist. To do this, you'll want to come up with a secondary or complimentary interest, passion, or skill that would go really well alongside your primary area to differentiate yourself from the crowd. For example, you may love sports, but you also love photography. You decide that you want to combine the two and do sports photography for local youth organizations. That gives you a unique specialty in your area, thus giving your work focus and making you stand out to those who need that specific skill set. This is a great way to use a more traditional path even when you're multi-passionate because you're framing your passions around a model that gives more dimensionality to what you do. It's not only about the one specific skill that you have but instead becomes an integration of your talents in a way that gives you a leg up.

With this strategy of combining two tangential skill sets, you start to weed out the competition and essentially make them non-existent within the space you want to be working. Have you heard of the blue ocean and the red ocean before? In the book, *Blue Ocean Strategy*, your market is compared to an ocean where you need to compete for fish.[71] If there is a lot of competition for the same customers, then it's essentially shark-infested waters full of red blood and hungry competitors trying to get the fish for themselves. However, if you create your own little blue ocean based around your own specific offers and expertise, then you establish yourself in a market all your own. You essentially get rid of all the competition because no one does exactly what you do or provides the same value you provide.[72] This is what you want to accomplish here when you combine skill sets with a primary and secondary interest. You create that blue ocean for yourself that will get you much farther than if you were competing with all the rest of the sharks in doing the same thing for the same audience.

Now, you don't just want to stop there, though. You want to keep going with integrating your interests and passions along with continuing to make sure you are not competing with anyone in the marketplace. This is where you take it to the next level and bring in even more of your passions as tertiary elements to your business. These are the ones that are going to shape your customer experience and make it as memorable as possible. You want to incorporate things that are unique to

---

[71] Kim, W. C., & Mauborgne, R. (2005). *Blue ocean strategy: How to create uncontested market space and make the competition irrelevant*. Boston, Mass: Harvard Business School Press.
[72] Kim, W. C., & Mauborgne, R. (2005). *Blue ocean strategy: How to create uncontested market space and make the competition irrelevant*. Boston, Mass: Harvard Business School Press.

you and that your customers would love. It could be that you love making healthy snacks, so you provide an entire photo session experience for a sports team and provide homemade healthy treats after you take their pictures. It could be that you love graphic design, so in addition to doing a sports team's photos you also design custom team banners and flags to be sold to fans at the games. In each of these ways, you're able to create a more memorable and enriching experience for your customers that shows you care about more than just your primary job. You actually care about making them happy and giving them a great experience from working with you.

To help you understand this primary purpose business model further, here's another metaphor. Assume this business framework is like our planetary orbit within space. Your core message that you chose in a previous chapter is the sun. The role you play in presenting that message, whether it be as creator, innovator, or any other one, is the path you choose to take in revolving around the sun. Your primary interest area that you're pursuing in your business is Earth revolving around your sun's core message, and it's the place where all of your content and offerings live. So your primary interest or skill (Earth) is traveling along the path synonymous with the role you've chosen and revolving around your core message (the sun). In addition to that, you have your moon that revolves around Earth. The moon is where you have your complimentary passions and interests that support the Earth to create an experience for your customers.

Think about this all in combination with each other for a moment. If we didn't have the sun, how would we function on Earth? It probably wouldn't be very well with no light, and we surely wouldn't be able to grow much here. The same is true in your business without a core message. What about the moon? The moon has powerful energy behind it that greatly impacts our weather and climate here on Earth. You can apply this directly to the complementary interests that you bring into your business. They'll greatly impact the feeling and positioning of your business and therefore play a large role in the way you're able to connect with your audience and shape your offers. Without all of these elements at play together, your business would be very one-dimensional. Your goal instead should be to amplify this interchange to a point where you're able to create your own blue ocean strategy in the marketplace.

I know I'm mixing metaphors here a bit, but I want you to understand that your passions are not mutually exclusive. They can work quite well together if you take the time to plan out how they revolve around each other to give your audience what it needs and wants. Keep telling yourself that you have been given the exact right gifts and experiences to be able to live purposefully and make the impact that only you can. There's nothing you've been through or have learned by accident. It's all put you right where you need to be in order to share

your message with the world. In saying that, all you
need to do is to tap into your own gifts. You can create a
unique experience for your community by being flexible
enough to intertwine the things you love. Get out of the
mindset that one primary purpose is the only thing that
drives your business model to success. It's not. What
does is your ability to take that and transform it into a
unique and complete experience unlike any other.

Aside from using multiple passions here to create an
amazing customer experience, it also serves you well by
keeping you motivated day to day. You'll have the ability to lean more on certain passions over others day to
day dependent upon your mood and inspiration. One of
the biggest reasons I've chosen to present this as a good
business model for multi-passionates is that it doesn't
restrict you to continuous focus on one subject all the
time. You can use different productivity and management skills to switch back and forth between projects
and tasks, thus keeping you from having that internal
alarm clock going off when you're bored. For example,
one week you may choose to focus on doing photo sessions while the next week you work on your website
and graphic design. You have flexibility built in here to
shift gears more easily when you need it.

Overall, this experiential framework is a good choice if
you're the type of person that wants to stick to tried-
and-true methods. If you don't want to go too far off the
beaten path but love the idea of reframing the business
norm into something more tailored, then this is for you.

Give yourself some grace when it comes to choosing what your primary purpose will be, though. It may take some trial and error to get something that you feel comfortable with enough to work on consistently. Don't feel pressured to stick to it if you're getting the urge to move on. In the beginning, testing is all you need to be doing, and you need to listen to your gut when it tells you it's time for a change. If you start to make traction in an area, though, you've got to give yourself some time to see how it pans out. That's the only way you'll see growth. Set a time limit for yourself that you can handle and see what results you get in that set amount of time. If everything is clicking and your work is resonating with your ideal audience, then keep what works and integrate another passion into your business to develop that customer experience even further.

One thing I will say about utilizing this method is that you need to continually put yourself in the shoes of your customers. Ask yourself if you're providing the experience that they'll truly love or if you're adding too many unnecessary things into the mix? You don't want to go overboard with adding twenty different elements into your business. That will make you as well as your followers confused. In this case, some of your interests may serve you better staying as personal interests. Stick to about two or three at most that you'll incorporate into your customer experience. Create a checks and balance system for yourself to evaluate whether you are in fact enhancing the experience for customers every time you integrate something new. Make a list of questions to ask yourself about how they'll feel when they come across that component of your business. Will it increase their ability to achieve something? Will it make working with you more fun and enjoyable? Will it build more trust with your tribe? Always bring your focus back to the emotions that you're creating in your tribe with the experience you create. That will make this a successful framework for you as well as your customers when you can leave them excited to work with you again and again.

Action Exercise:

Here's where you're going to delineate the components of your experiential business framework. To create your framework, take the exercise from the previous chapter where you made a list of all of your strengths and experiences. You're going to use this now as you nail down which area you want to be the primary focal point of your business. This will be the thing that you're known for and will be very closely aligned to your core message. Thus, you'll want to choose something that goes hand-in-hand with that message and that people will naturally connect to it without having to overthink it.

For example, if your core message is that you want mothers to practice self care, and you have a skill set in being a doula, then you may just choose to have your primary practice be doula services. This is a very self-

explanatory connection that doesn't require much thinking to connect the dots. It's an easily identifiable service
that makes sense in the context of your message.

On the other hand, you may choose to do something
very unlikely as a primary focus to pair up with your core
message. Your core message could be that community
service is an important part of society. When people
think of community service, they don't usually think of
CEOs, but you may have business training and choose
to focus your attention on mentoring CEOs in incorporating service into their companies. You're making more of
a stretch here to connect the dots between service and
profit, but yet you can make it work and have it serve as
a unique twist. Unlikely combinations can really set you
apart in the marketplace if you do it in a way that appeals to your audience well.

To do this exercise, give yourself at least ten minutes to
sit and brainstorm with your list of strengths and experiences. Go down your list and put a star next to anything
that you feel could stand alone as a business to solve
someone's problem or help your audience in some way.
Once you have those starred items, write them each
along the top of another sheet of paper. Then, go down
your list of strengths and experiences again, but this
time look for things that are complementary to your
starred items. Which ones would work well to enhance
the others? Draw branch lines out beneath each of your
starred items, and write the items below it that are complementary to each one. Do this until you have at least
two or three complimentary items under each starred
item.

Now, look at the branched list that you've created. Which of the starred items and its complementary components most appeals to you? Which is the easiest to get started with? Which would be the most lucrative? Which one makes you feel expansive and excited to get started? Give each one a rating from one to five based on each of these questions, and review the one that has gotten the highest rating from you. How does it make you feel to think about that one as your business model? Let it percolate a bit and envision yourself doing something within that subject area every day. Think about how you would use the complementary interests to make it a unique experience. Does it seem like something you'd love?

Take some time to review your list further and think about this exercise. Remember how you felt about each of the items as you wrote them and thought about doing them. The way you felt will once again give you a big clue into how well they'd fit you and if you'd be excited enough about them to make a business grow over time. Only you can decide what's right for you, but you'll have help when you need it if you just tap into what your gut is telling you right off the bat. Listening to it here will set you off in the right direction to start.

If you're thinking that setting up a business based around a primary purpose and an experience just isn't going to do it for you, then I've got another solution for you. In this one, you establish your own personal brand, meaning you are what people buy into here. It's along the same lines as having a portfolio as in the creator role that we discussed in the last chapter. You create a brand around yourself and your personality with your core message being the central focus of everything you do. Even if you choose to provide services rather than products, this can be a great way to go as the face of your company. When you are the one running the show, wearing all the hats, and doing all the work in front of your tribe as well as behind the scenes, then you will be the one that your audience needs to relate to and connect with at every level. That's what makes this such a powerful model in that you're building a foundational relationship out of that integral emotional connection with your people. From there, you build your know, like, and trust factor and deliver what your tribe wants.

In order to make this effective, you'll need to have a central platform around which you build your work. That platform could be a podcast, YouTube videos, books, local workshops, or anything you choose. It's a way to put your message out there in a very accessible way that allows people to test you out and see if your brand is for them. If you do this well and get your personality and message across right away, it should be very clear to them whether they belong in your tribe or not. This way you'll weed out those who aren't your ideal customers very quickly so you can focus on building connections with those who are.

Your platform is something you want to choose early on and start creating content for immediately, but you can always change directions if you find that one space isn't working well for you. This is something I've played around with in my own career. I've tested out having a blog, YouTube channel, podcasting, and now books. Each platform has its own pros and cons, and you need to give whichever one you choose some time to work before you decide if it's right for you or not. The time period for testing could be anywhere from a month to six months dependent upon your brand and what you do. Just be aware that it takes time to see if you like the way it feels to present information in these different ways and whether your audience responds best to one over another. If for any reason you've tried one platform for awhile and it's just not your cup of tea, pivot and move on to test another.

To give you some context here, let's look at the Martha Stewart brand again. She created a massive brand around personal touches that she's used in all of her work, and it's spanned across so many different areas including events, food, and handmade projects.[73] The company has now become a lifestyle brand, and when people think of the Martha Stewart label, they know it's synonymous with something made with care and a detailed touch. Her brand character also portrays this in all of the design elements as well. You can feel a hand-

---

[73] Duncan, Melanie. (2013). "Case Study- Martha Stewart: How to Build a Personal Brand." Retrieved from http://www.entrepreneuressacademy.com/blog/case-study-martha-stewart/

made, homey quality to it all as you interact with the website, read the magazine, watch the television show, or engage with any of the other brand components.

You have to be mindful of how you're making everything go together when you create a personal brand. It's important to be consistent with the character and personality that you're displaying across all of your content, marketing, products, and services. That way people can very easily identify the personality of the brand and whether that suits them or not. It's important to also note here that this is where you want to distinguish your audience clearly. If you haven't already done the ideal customer exercises in chapter four, then go back to that section and make sure you're clear on who you're serving.

When it comes to consistently showing the character of your brand, it's best to identify with a certain group of people who will resonate with that vibe. I'm sure you've heard plenty of business experts say, "If you try to serve everyone, you'll end up serving no one." That's because speaking someone's language allows you to essentially get inside their head and come across as though you're reading their mind. They'll think you know exactly what's bothering them and what they need and want to make it better. Because of that, they'll look to you as the person to solve their problems. Then, it'll become so much easier for you when you've identified what your audience specifically likes, what brand characteristics and qualities attract them, and how your personality fits well with them. If you can match those things up well, you have the ability to build your know, like, and trust factor substantially by authentically showing up as someone who gets them right off the bat.

Putting personality into your brand is such a critical component here that it's important to note that you want to make your brand characteristics equate to your personality. In the next action exercise, I'll walk you through how to determine your brand characteristics. These should largely be taken from your natural characteristics. If you are a bold, daring, and adventurous person, then your personal brand should reflect that. If you are quiet, reserved, and introspective, then your brand should feel more calming and serene. Being able to pair your personality with that of your brand just takes a little planning. Once you've nailed down specific adjectives to define your brand from the exercise, it becomes all about the presentation. How will you convey those characteristics in your content? What will you show your audience to set a scene that gives the same feeling? In what ways will you display your own personality as the face of the brand? Those are the things you must think about as your integrate yourself into your business.

As your audience interacts with your brand, it should feel like they're home. When your ideal customer comes to your website for the first time or sees your social media profiles, that person should feel like they instantly belong. To give them that feeling, you have to ensure that the photos you display, the videos you present, and the copy on the pages really speaks to them directly and no one else. Remember, you only have about eight seconds or so to gain someone's interest and make them want to dig a little deeper.[74] After that, they'll bounce away if they don't see something that's right for them. If you're trying to create something that appeals to everyone, it will fall flat and not really resonate with anyone in particular. This is why you want to try your best to focus your attention on creating an authentic brand character that really speaks to what your brand is all about and has a clear customer avatar in mind.

Once you've chosen your main platform and figured out how to integrate your personality into your branding, you want to start developing your body of work. Refer to your core message and the exercise in the previous chapter regarding your strengths to determine the best ways to solve your target audience's problems, make an impact in your chosen field, or create change. Be as specific as you can about the projects that you feel will best represent your message and talents. This could be anything from writing a fiction book series to creating a collection of handmade products. Lay out your project ideas fully and see which ones are the easiest to start with and which ones require much more time to put

---

[74] Conran, Joshua. (2014. October 13). "How to Grab Your Target's Attention in 8 Seconds (Or Less)." Retrieved from https://www.inc.com/joshua-conran/how-to-grab-your-target-s-attention-in-8-seconds-or-less.html

together. You'll want to employ some prioritization skills here and initially devote your time to those with the biggest bang for your buck. Essentially, that will be the ones that are easiest for you to do right away and the ones with the biggest return either monetarily, through traffic to your business, or by making an impact. You can slowly build up to completing larger projects, but give yourself at least a couple quick accomplishments to start with if you can. That way you'll build confidence, momentum, and interest in your work.

Action Exercise:

Whether you choose to use an experiential model for your business or a personal brand, you'll want to give your brand character a little more structure. If you haven't guessed it by now, I'm a big fan of structure, especially for multi-passionate people. Without it, you'll be floundering around with way too many possibilities. If you just set a few simple limits to give you a little bit of a guide, you'll be setting yourself up for success much more so than aimlessly wandering from one idea to the next. That's why in this exercise, I'm going to give you more guidance on how to create the feeling of your brand to draw in your ideal customers.

Take at least ten minutes to sit quietly and brainstorm. The goal is to determine three to five adjectives that define your brand. You'll want to be clear about the vibe you want to create because this is something that will carry through in every single thing you create and put out in the world. Use your own personality and innate qualities to draw upon but also think about what you want your business to represent to others. It's important that emotion is connected to the adjectives you choose in some way. Evoking emotion is what will resonate with your ideal customer and have them continue thinking about you and how they felt about your message.

Make a list of all the things that come to mind to describe your personality as well as what you do. You want to be expressive about your personality in terms of friendliness, boldness, or even meditativeness. Then, include items about the end result that people get from working with you and the benefits they'll receive. This might include things like being fulfilling, freeing, or rejuvenating. If any of those things are what you want to bring out in your brand, then include them in your list.

Now, nail down your top three characteristics. These should be the absolute priority for you to get across in your content. These are the things that get to the core of what your brand represents and how it feels to your audience. Write your final three to five selections on the bottom of your paper or note-taking area. You now have your brand character and can start creating all of the elements of your brand around this. If you already have a business, then take this time to reevaluate whether the adjectives you wrote down are representative of the brand you're already building. If something is lacking, then take a step back and assess from a bird's eye view to see where there are places to make adjustments to get back in line with these characteristics. Remember, using these adjectives as your guide in content creation will make it easier to connect with your ideal audience and show them that they belong. It's your job to convey these feelings throughout your brand so that people understand where you're coming from each time they see you.

Whether you've chosen to go the route of an experiential business or to build a personal brand, you still have to tie everything together and give it a consistent feel. The first way you do that is with your core messaging. That message and underlying intent of what you do should carry through in some way, shape, or form throughout your work. After that, the character of your brand plays a large role. The branding world actually has its own set of archetypes that they use to classify a business' approach to its brand persona. It's a lot like a person because you're defining these qualities just as if someone would look for these qualities in a friend or a mate. The same is true here in looking for brands that you can relate to and eventually trust enough to do business with.

Once you have chosen your business model, it's time to decide on how you'll approach your branding. Here's where you get to choose from a variety of different options again. You may find that one or two of these stand out the most to you, and it's perfectly fine to combine a couple of them together. Mixing a couple of these is a nice way to show off a little dimensionality as a multi-passionate entrepreneur. I would suggest, though, that you try to stay within the realm of just one to two here so as not to confuse yourself or your audience. Basically, you're going to use these to shape the character of your brand, right alongside your personality and the adjectives you chose. They should all go hand in hand, and knowing each of these will make it a whole lot easier to create content and even products for your market.

Some of the brand archetypes may be a bit more straightforward than others, so refer to the examples of the companies that exemplify each one if you need to clarify any of them. It may take you a bit of time to pinpoint which one would work best for you and your audience. On the other hand, you may know immediately that one or two of them will just click for you and feel right. Don't second guess yourself if that happens. It's usually best to go with your initial instinct especially on something like brand character that is going to be so closely related to the personality you want to exude with your business.

To start, let's look at the magician brand. This brand type is all about establishing yourself as a visionary or about bringing dreams to life in some way.[75] As we've mentioned previously, Disney is the perfect example of this

---

[75] Gabor, Deb. (2017, May 25). "The 12 Brand Archetypes-Which is Yours?" Retrieved from http://www.cobizmag.com/Business-Insights/The-12-brand-archetypes--Which-is-yours/

brand archetype as they are all about the imagination and making dreams come true.[76] Think about the Disney movies you know with princes and princesses, fairies, castles, and even magic. They really want to inspire fantasies and a world of possibilities. If you choose this as your brand archetype, you'll want everything to have a magical, imaginative, or even spiritual quality to it. This may be right for you if you're considering a market geared toward children, self-improvement, or even spirituality. Those subjects all have a bit of an ethereal feel associated with them already, so combining those with a magical style would make sense.

The sage brand is one focused on knowledge, wisdom, and intelligence.[77] It encompasses thriving for truth and constant learning. Some great examples of brands like this include Harvard University, the British Broadcasting Corporation (BBC), and the Public Broadcasting Service (PBS).[78] If you think about each one of those, you can tell that they are all synonymous with spreading knowledge and furthering education. To build a brand like this, you'll want to focus on learning as key. You might

---

[76] Gabor, Deb. (2017, May 25). "The 12 Brand Archetypes-Which is Yours?" Retrieved from http://www.cobizmag.com/Business-Insights/The-12-brand-archetypes--Which-is-yours/

[77] The Hartford. (2018). "The 12 Brand Archetypes." Retrieved from https://www.thehartford.com/business-playbook/in-depth/choosing-brand-archetype

[78] The Hartford. (2018). "The 12 Brand Archetypes." Retrieved from https://www.thehartford.com/business-playbook/in-depth/choosing-brand-archetype

choose to include a lot of workshops or even use author-ship as your main platform. It would also be a good idea to present your content with a teaching tone or even one where facts are important to the role you play. If you've chosen to assume an idealist role or one as a curator, then branding that goes with the sage archetype would work really well to define the learning aspect of your brand.

Next is the innocent brand archetype. This one consists of purity and innocence just like it sounds.[79] To use this in your branding, you would give everything a tone of gentleness, morality, or even simplicity. The company, Dove, is a great example where you can see the inno-cence in their marketing and the purity of their images.[80] If you're interested in doing something in a children's related field or even something regarding health, this might be a good choice for your brand persona. Also, if you're taking on a role of an idealist, this would go well with the vibe of that depending on the cause you're working toward.

What about if you're a bit bolder and more wild at heart? Then, you should be going for the outlaw arche-

<hr>

[79] The Hartford. (2018). "The 12 Brand Archetypes." Retrieved from https://www.thehartford.com/business-playbook/in-depth/choosing-brand-archetype
[80] The Hartford. (2018). "The 12 Brand Archetypes." Retrieved from https://www.thehartford.com/business-playbook/in-depth/choosing-brand-archetype

type. The outlaw is rebellious, wild, and goes against authority.[81] I've seen many people using this one in the entrepreneurial world these days, but if it fits your personality, then go with it. You've got to really own this one and be willing to push it. Play around with it as much as you can to make your brand feel edgy and different. Some great examples of this one can be seen in Harley Davidson or the Virgin brand where they both give off that rebellious vibe and resisting the norm.[82] As a creator or a thought leader, this would be a great brand persona to use. It would emphasize that you're not afraid to stand out and be heard in what you do and that you're willing to push against typical ways of thinking. Just be sure that it truly makes sense for who you are as a person so that you're being authentic to yourself and your message.

Another one that is just like it sounds is the jester. This archetype is fun, humorous, and light-hearted.[83] Brands like this are all about making things funny and giving their audience a good laugh in the process of whatever they do. Some examples of this type of brand include

---

[81] The Hartford. (2018). "The 12 Brand Archetypes." Retrieved from https://www.thehartford.com/business-playbook/in-depth/choosing-brand-archetype

[82] The Hartford. (2018). "The 12 Brand Archetypes." Retrieved from https://www.thehartford.com/business-playbook/in-depth/choosing-brand-archetype

[83] Gabor, Deb. (2017, May 25). "The 12 Brand Archetypes-Which is Yours?" Retrieved from http://www.cobizmag.com/Business-Insights/The-12-brand-archetypes--Which-is-yours/

Ben and Jerry's ice cream and Old Spice. Each of these uses humor in their advertising to make their customers laugh a bit at the brand.[84] You can most certainly incorporate branding like this into any role that you play, but it's probably best for the less serious roles such as a curator or a creator. If you try to be a jester as an idealist or a thought leader for serious issues, you may get a lot of strange looks. Then again, that might just be what people need to reframe their perspectives. Be careful that you're using this one appropriately and that once again your own personality reflects the same sense of humor and lightheartedness that you want to build into the brand.

What about if you're a more heartfelt person? Then, you want to go with the lover brand. This brand archetype is warm, passionate, and romantic even.[85] These brands are often about building relationships. Hallmark can be considered a great brand in this category that is all about sincerity, love, and creating bonding memories through their cards and gifts. On the other end of the spectrum, you can see Victoria's Secret as a very romantic brand.

---

[84] Gabor, Deb. (2017, May 25). "The 12 Brand Archetypes-Which is Yours?" Retrieved from http://www.cobizmag.com/Business-Insights/The-12-brand-archetypes--Which-is-yours/
[85] The Hartford. (2018). "The 12 Brand Archetypes." Retrieved from https://www.thehartford.com/business-playbook/in-depth/choosing-brand-archetype

It's all about playing up the sensuality of the brand.[86] Even when they do their big annual fashion show, the company always makes it a point to play up the romance and passion for its products. If you're the type of person who tends to lead from the heart and you're interested in providing elements of love, family bonding, or even romance in your work, then definitely give this brand persona a try.

If you're all about being adventurous or exploring new things, then the explorer archetype might be right up your alley.[87] This brand persona deals with independence and discovery and comes across with a sense of freedom. This one is great for travel, coaching, or anything that deals with getting out and exploring more of the world or even yourself. Companies like Jeep and REI are both great examples of how you can create the feeling of exploration and adventure in the way you put together your marketing campaigns.[88] Both show a lot of outdoor activities in the scenes they display whether it be with a Jeep bounding over hills or with an image of a rock climber wearing gear from REI. Those visuals are

---

[86] The Hartford. (2018). "The 12 Brand Archetypes." Retrieved from https://www.thehartford.com/business-playbook/in-depth/choosing-brand-archetype

[87] The Hartford. (2018). "The 12 Brand Archetypes." Retrieved from https://www.thehartford.com/business-playbook/in-depth/choosing-brand-archetype

[88] The Hartford. (2018). "The 12 Brand Archetypes." Retrieved from https://www.thehartford.com/business-playbook/in-depth/choosing-brand-archetype

very easily tied to getting out and discovering new things and automatically instill a feeling of freedom in the viewer. If you'd like to use a similar approach in your own business, it would work well for aspirational subjects along the lines of finding your purpose, seeing the world, or creating a location-independent lifestyle. You could also build it into a product-based business successfully if what you're offering is geared toward travel or the outdoors.

Let's look at one that comes across as very organized and even methodical. The ruler brand style is great for those who are on the type-A side and like the idea of control.[89] This archetype is really big on responsibility and leadership as well as giving a sense of stability. You can see that former First Lady, Senator, and Secretary of State, Hillary Clinton, has a ruler style when it comes to how she's presented in the public eye. She has an authoritative presence that exudes professionalism and shows she values responsibility highly. A company that displays this quite well is the Rolex watch brand. Their advertising shows sophisticated people who have reached a level of status and achievement. The company's products are often featured at prestigious sporting events and tournaments signifying the high-level positioning and achievement.[90] If you have chosen to play a

---

[89] Brand Personalities. (2018). "The Ruler." Retrieved from https://brandpersonalities.com.au/personalities/the-ruler/
[90] Brand Personalities. (2018). "The Ruler." Retrieved from https://brandpersonalities.com.au/personalities/the-ruler/

role as an innovator, then this may be a good choice if you're interested in creating order out of chaos. You may also assume this branding style if you're a thought leader and are always on the ball when it comes to the way you organize, manage, and lead your tribe.

Now can you think of some brands that are more nurturing rather than being so rigid? Children's brands such as Pampers or even Johnson and Johnson are great examples of caregiver brands.[91] These are brands that are more compassionate and use their advertising to show a nurturing scene, just as how Pampers and Johnson and Johnson show parents taking care of small children in a very gentle and loving way with bath time and diapering products.The idea here is to come across as selfless and caring about others above all else. You can apply this to a variety of different subjects that you may not necessarily think about at first, but because you can always show how you care about your customers, it can work.

Take for instance, the car company, Volvo, and how they're all about safety and security for their customers.[92] You would buy a Volvo if you were in the

[91] Gabor, Deb. (2017, May 25). "The 12 Brand Archetypes-Which is Yours?" Retrieved from http://www.cobizmag.com/Business-Insights/The-12-brand-archetypes--Which-is-yours/
[92] Brand Personalities. (2018). "The Caregiver." Retrieved from https://brandpersonalities.com.au/personalities/the-caregiver/

market for something that you knew would keep your family safe and sound on the road. That's because they've done a good job in developing a brand around the strong principles of taking care of the people who drive their cars.[93] To put this into practice yourself, you want to make sure that your personality is more gentle and easy-going rather than overbearing. If you work with parents or in fields with families, this is a great fit right off the bat. It's also perfect for idealists with a message associated with health and wellness or self-care. However, if you want to incorporate this brand style into any business you're thinking about creating, then start by focusing on being nurturing toward your customers and always showing how you take care of them in what you do.

Hero brands are pretty self-explanatory. They display a sense of strength, courage, and confidence.[94] Nike is an excellent example as they advertise with many images about endurance and believing in yourself. Much of their tag-lines and marketing campaigns display scenes where athletes are digging deep to get across the finish line or pushing themselves to work harder. They're all about victory through determination.[95] If you have a

---

[93] Brand Personalities. (2018). "The Caregiver." Retrieved from https://brandpersonalities.com.au/personalities/the-caregiver/

[94] Brand Personalities. (2018). "The Hero." Retrieved from https://brandpersonalities.com.au/personalities/the-hero/

[95] Brand Personalities. (2018). "The Hero." Retrieved from https://brandpersonalities.com.au/personalities/the-hero/

background in the military or if you've served in some capacity, you may want to incorporate a piece of this style into your own brand. Subjects such as sports and anything competitive also go hand-in-hand with this archetype because they both reference that feeling of striving to be better than you are currently. Using this style can really help your audience to understand your background, where you've come from, and what you've struggled with. It can help them to very clearly see that you've been in their shoes and come out the other side, and it will go a long way in building your know, like, and trust factor quickly.

Now, what if you feel like you're just a regular person and that you've got something to share with everyone? I've got to say, that while I don't recommend you go this route, there is a place for it. You can use the brand persona of a regular guy or girl to show inclusion, connectivity, and support.[96] The best way to play this one up in your business is to use it by creating a feeling of trustworthiness and belonging so that your ideal customers get a sense that they're in the right place for them. This is a much better approach than actually trying to be for everyone, which is extremely difficult to market. Rather, you want to show people that you're down to earth, and they'll easily fit into your community. Folgers coffee

---

[96] Gabor, Deb. (2017, May 25). "The 12 Brand Archetypes-Which is Yours?" Retrieved from http://www.cobizmag.com/Business-Insights/The-12-brand-archetypes--Which-is-yours/

does this well with their brand of inclusion.[97] Their idea is that if you're a coffee drinker, Folgers is for you. It's not something just for hip urbanites or for the earthy, hippie crowd. The brand works for people who just want a simple cup of coffee that they can trust is good.[98] Taking this idea of simplicity and belonging, you can use the "girl next door" approach and show your tribe that you can relate to them on their level. This one might be good if you're trying to be in a leadership role such as a thought leader. You can use this style to show your audience that you're just like them and understand their point of view.

The final brand archetype that we'll cover here is the creator. The creator style is very much along the same lines as the role of being a creator that we talked about previously, although the archetype here is where you actually portray yourself as being creative or artistic. This means that rather than the act of creating work, here you are displaying the qualities of an artist or creative in your brand. The goal is for your brand to feel expressive, unique, and artsy through your use of visuals, copy, and marketing efforts that give off that vibe.[99]

[97] Gabor, Deb. (2017, May 25). "The 12 Brand Archetypes-Which is Yours?" Retrieved from http://www.cobizmag.com/Business-Insights/The-12-brand-archetypes--Which-is-yours/
[98] Gabor, Deb. (2017, May 25). "The 12 Brand Archetypes-Which is Yours?" Retrieved from http://www.cobizmag.com/Business-Insights/The-12-brand-archetypes--Which-is-yours/
[99] Brand Personalities. (2018). "The Creator." Retrieved from https://brandpersonalities.com.au/personalities/the-creator/

Basically, you want to overemphasize that you're a creative person. Lego and Crayola are the quintessential creator brands. They both represent the idea of inventiveness with lots of possibility and creativity.[100] You can definitely bring this into your business if you lean toward having a portfolio of work as in the creator role. If you're choosing to play another role such as a curator, just add in elements that are synonymous with creativity. That may be bold splashes of color, well-designed fonts and graphic elements, or even a handmade feel. You can always give off the vibe of creativity if it suits you well and that's how you approach your work.

Now that I've gone through some options for business frameworks and developing your brand character, you should have a solid understanding of how you can build a brand that works with your multi-passionate approach. It's completely your choice if you prefer to develop a business with an experiential model or to create a personal brand. They are each solid choices and suited for different needs. Either way should give you the flexibility you need to work on a variety of different interests and not reach the level of boredom we all tend to reach by doing one thing for too long.

---

[100] Brand Personalities. (2018). "The Creator." Retrieved from https://brandpersonalities.com.au/personalities/the-creator/

Giving your brand a personality is a major component in making your business model come alive for your audience. It gives it more dimensionality and helps you convey that it's an extension of you, the owner and face of the company, rather than just an organization that's meant to make money. You don't want to just choose a business model and start creating products or services. No one will connect with that. Personality is key to developing relationships you need to make your business successful and grow. Without this element, your business will fall flat and not develop the emotional connection that draws people in and helps them see the value in your work.

If you can pair your own personality traits and the adjectives you've chosen for your brand with the brand archetypes that I've outlined, you'll have a solid way of presenting your unique vibe in the marketplace to set you apart from others. This will also give you something to shoot for when you create consistent content that feels cohesive across all of your platforms or offerings. You'll be able to come up with ideas around the specific emotions you want to create in your images, copy, and in your marketing campaigns. This way you'll know the feelings you're creating will be seen over and over with your brand, thus driving home the point of your brand being synonymous with those emotions. In addition, you'll be giving your audience something to long for or aspire to...something that they could only get if they worked with you.

As you further develop your brand and decide what works well and what doesn't, you can make changes and reassess whether it all fits into your big vision. Just keep in mind that your core message, your business framework, and your brand style should all work together to create a unique way for you to stand out in the marketplace. Plus, it takes you showing up authentically as who you are. Now, there are so many ways to combine all of those elements, so the way you choose to do it will be unlike anyone else. It's up to you to find the right balance and intertwine each component in a way that makes sense for you and your audience.

Use your many gifts, areas of expertise, and experience to shape your brand into something that lights you up and makes you feel like it's an extension of yourself. After all, you are the face of the company, and you'll be the reason people will choose to do business with you. They won't make their decision based solely on your product or offer. In the end, it'll most likely come down to how much they resonate with you as a person and what your brand stands for. That's why you've got to be thoughtful about the way you represent yourself and make sure everything you put out into the world is synonymous with your vibe, your message, and your vision.

Chapter Seven

Moving Forward

You should now understand how to create focus in your business when you've got a plethora of passions. The next step is figuring out how to move forward and stick to what you're working on long enough to grow. I know as a multi-passionate person myself, this is a lot easier said than done. That's why I want to use this final chapter to give you some strategies that have worked for me in my business endeavors as well as in the projects I've managed professionally to keep me on track for success.

The biggest things that you've already got to help you with this are your big vision for what you want to achieve, your core driving message that always should feel right to you, and your business framework that ties your interests together. Using these in conjunction with each other will allow you to move back and forth among tasks and projects so that no two days have to be the same if you don't want them to be. Essentially, you have the flexibility to get things done as needed while giving yourself a much less constraining way of doing it. That feeling of not being confined or boxed in can be really freeing when you're testing out new ideas and projects to build up your brand.

Just to make sure you've got the boredom under control, I'm going to give you two project management strategies that will help you change things up enough to feel like you're doing everything you want to be doing. They'll also give you the ability to make progress on what you want to accomplish rather than continuing to be stuck because you can't decide where to focus your attention. I've seen these work for many entrepreneurs who are building their businesses on their own and wearing many hats. I've also used them first-hand for large-scale organizational projects that have seen huge success. At their most basic level, these are processes that help you devote your attention to your specific priorities. On a grander scale, they allow you to work on what inspires you to maximize your time in getting closer to your big vision for success.

The first management process that I want to share with you is called Batching. You may have heard the term before or even used it as part of the systems you use to get things done. Batching is basically where you set aside certain chunks of time to group like tasks together. You may decide to do this in hour-long blocks, half-day blocks, or full days of time. I recommend at least full or half day blocks for your business tasks if possible. That way you can fully get into a flow of work during that time and batch together your tasks for a month at a time into one session. Plus, it'll give you the ability to wrap your head around what you need to be doing to move forward. You can use the same days every single week to get the same work done or at the very least know how to lump like tasks together for more efficiency.

Let me give you an example. If you know you need to work on graphic design for your website, social media images, and marketing campaigns, then you might choose to lump all of those together on Tuesdays as your "graphic design day." Then, you may decide that you need a day every week to focus solely on doing creative work like painting or photography. You could make Fridays your creative day where you know each week that you'll have that specific time set aside to devote to those interests. By scheduling your time this way, you're designating your own priorities and making sure that you're as efficient as possible in accomplishing them.

What makes this batching technique so effective is that you get into a zone while you work on one specific task, and the momentum builds as you keep going with that one thing. You may have a system for doing your graphics or putting your social media posts together. When you sit down to batch your tasks, you just go through that workflow with one job after the other, so it becomes a repetitive task that's easier to do once you're in the groove of it. One thing that will also make you much more efficient with this technique is to ensure that you're not being interrupted by any other tasks, messages, or meetings during your batching time. You should have one sole focus. This will give you clarity in what you're doing without distraction from the task at hand.

The way you choose to implement this is entirely up to you and how often you need to do your tasks. You can set it up to have batching time weekly, monthly, or even every year if you'd like. For instance, the mundane tasks like social media scheduling or writing your email newsletters could be batched together every month or even every week if necessary. However, you might choose to do your yearly planning and financial budgeting during a full two-day session only once or twice a year. It really depends on what you need to get done and what the appropriate timeline is for those things.

As far as how this strategy works for multi-passionate people, I have to say that it really does give you that nice balance of planning and flexibility. You're able to lay the groundwork for yourself and know that you've got time devoted to accomplishing everything you want to work on in your business and life. However, because you've grouped like tasks with other like tasks, you have the ability to move those batch times around as you see fit. If one day you feel like doing something different than what you had originally planned, then you just exchange one batch task day for another. I do this a lot with my own schedule. Some days I have scheduled for full writing days whereas others I'll be doing all video editing. If there's a day that I had planned to be doing writing, and I just don't feel up to it, I'll usually listen to my gut and change that batch time out with the editing time. This is perfectly fine so long as no tasks are overdue or coming up on a deadline.

Another beautiful thing about this method is that you get to change what you're focusing on every day if you'd like. This is a revelation for multi-passionate people because you're always doing something different, and that's built into the systems of your business. One day could be artistic while the next day is about marketing. You could even choose to only work three days a week on business-related tasks and then devote every other day of the week to doing things with your kids and family. That's completely your prerogative, and if you try it out one way but don't like it, then the system is very easily changed.

In order to implement this in your own business, you'll want to figure out the best timeline for yourself, the categories of tasks that you'd like to prioritize, and how often you need to do all of your big task categories. Starting with your timeline, you may find that you need to do several things every single week, so outlining a weekly plan is a good idea. However, a lot of times, people prefer to work in monthly chunks of time. You may want to give this a try if you don't need things done as often as weekly, but you still need to maintain your business on a regular basis.

Then, you'll want to list out the major categories that you'd like to prioritize. This will depend highly on the work you do and what platform you've chosen to use to reach your audience. If you're a blogger, then you'll have lots of writing, editing, and marketing time to cover. If you're an artist that teaches in-person workshops, you'll most likely have more time devoted to creating your work, doing lesson plans, and also actually holding the workshops. Outline about three to five categories of tasks that make the most sense for what you do on a recurring basis, and those will be the primary emphasis for your batch days.

You also need to decide how often your tasks are typically due. Going back to the blogger example, you may be writing weekly blog posts and need to do your writing, editing, and social media marketing every single week based around when your posts need to be complete and go live. However, if you're an artist teaching workshops only once a month, then it may make more sense for you to break up your time monthly with specific days devoted to lesson planning or creation. Either way will work, but it has to make sense for how you have your deadlines set up in your business, how often events happen, or when your audience expects to hear from you.

For the sake of ease, I'm going to walk you through a way to plan your batching days for the week. You can still apply this to a monthly, quarterly, or other timeline based on your needs, but this is just to give you an idea of what I consider to be a best practice for this technique. To start, the way I've found to give yourself the most flexibility and the strongest push to actually get things done, is to plan a five-day workweek around batch days that are easily interchanged. Choose three batch days for three of the major categories that you'd like to prioritize and that need to happen on a regular basis. This may be your product creation, editing, coaching, or even marketing. Schedule your top three recurring categories for specific days of the week. I prefer Tuesday, Wednesday, and Thursday for these categories, but you can play around with the days that you like best. These days will become your "head down" days where you're focused on cranking out the work in these categories and getting stuff done.

Next, you want to make sure to give yourself time when you'll be able to do the work that's in your genius zone. This could be creative work such as photography, calligraphy, or sewing. However, if your genius zone is teaching, speaking, or something else action-oriented, then set aside a specific day for only this type of genius zone work. I prefer to set up this batch day on Fridays. By the end of the week, I usually just want to work on something that's simple and comes naturally to me or that makes me excited and inspired. This is the most important day of the week for you as a multi-passionate entrepreneur. It's the one that you absolutely must build into your schedule to keep you from feeling drained or overwhelmed. This is the day that allows you to completely focus on what you love and what you're good at to your core. Forget the mundane tasks for this day and just allow yourself to revel in the work you were born to do.

You should still have one more day of your work week that you need to account for, and in this outline, I want you to accommodate some time for planning. This is one you may not really think to schedule out and just tend to just fit in wherever you can. In all likelihood, when you get your business rolling and start to get busier, the first thing you're going to want to get rid of is your planning time. You need to resist the urge to do this, though, because you won't be able to move forward and grow if you don't give yourself a chance to figure out what direction to head in first. That's why my advice is to build in a day for planning on a regular basis so that you always have that time to check in with yourself and see if you're on the right path or if you need to make adjustments.

To do this, you'll want to use your batch day for planning to check in with your big vision first and make sure that what you're working on is in line with that. Think about whether the steps you're taking now make sense and what the next steps should be after that. When planning out your next steps, you could be considering things like what products to create, what offers your audience may like, or even what marketing strategies will get you to the next level. This is the time to look at the big picture and make sure you're preparing for it, as well as review the steps you're taking to get there.

I love the analogy of missing the forest for the trees. People say this when they talk about not being able to see the bigger picture because you're so far into the details of something. Don't get completely bogged down in the everyday details that you forget about your big picture. You always want to have your eye on the reason why you're doing all of this in the first place...in essence, your forest. By devoting recurring time to batch plan, you'll be setting yourself up right to constantly be on track to accomplishing your bigger goals.

As far as which day to utilize for planning, I tend to prefer Mondays for this. It's a great way to ease into the work week by just taking the time to think. You give yourself the boost you might need on a Monday to re-member your big vision for success and collect your thoughts regarding how things are going for your busi-ness. It's almost like a combination of a pep talk and a checks and balances day all in one. You've got the moti-vation gearing you up for a productive week by looking at your goals coupled with the ability to reflect on how things are going and where you might need to pivot. Covet this time highly in order to give you that much-needed gut check you'll need to keep progressing on a path that makes sense for you and your brand.

As far as putting all of those batch times together, this will give you a well-rounded way to approach prioritiz-ing your time. You'll end up with days devoted to work-ing in your various zones of genius which you can use for whichever subject you feel most drawn to at the moment. You'll have days set aside to work on maintaining your business and keeping up with the important tasks. Plus, you'll be ahead of the game with time set aside to get your plan together and know exactly where you're headed. That's a recipe for success wrapped up in an easy-to-implement system that caters to exactly what you need and want to accomplish.

Hopefully, by now you're feeling more confident about how to accomplish everything you want to achieve. There's one more system that I want to leave you with, though, because you still need to figure out what work actually deserves your attention. Before you move forward in any particular direction, you'll want to take at least a little bit of time (but not too much so that you're analyzing forever) to acknowledge the best uses of your inspiration, talents, experience, time, and resources. Basically, what are the things that you should be working on that will move you forward and how much time are you willing to devote to each one?

This is where you'll want to break down your big picture vision into smaller pieces and work backward. Thinking about everything you want to achieve may just overwhelm you to the point where you spin in circles not knowing where to start. If you're scheduling batch days without knowing why you're doing those things, then that isn't really going to help you in the long run.

You've got to be purposeful about what you're spending your time on to the point of almost having a checks and balance system for yourself. That way you'll know that everything you're doing is worthwhile, productive, and helping you to take action intentionally.

For this reason, I advocate for you to couple the batching strategy with this second technique of working on shorter project sprints. In agile project management, one of the approaches to this is called the Scrum Methodology.[101] This is where you utilize the idea of smaller sprint weeks to accomplish goals very quickly by devoting all of your attention to those specific projects.[102] It may be that your sprint lasts for one or two weeks, but you could also expand that if you've got something that would take a month or so. The point is that you keep your project small enough to be manageable in a short amount of time and that it becomes highly achievable when you can give a big push toward accomplishing it quickly.

If you have a clear vision for exactly what you're going after, this can be an incredibly effective way of getting

---

[101] Sliger, M. (2011). *Agile project management with Scrum*. Paper presented at PMI® Global Congress 2011—North America, Dallas, TX. Newtown Square, PA: Project Management Institute.

[102] Sliger, M. (2011). *Agile project management with Scrum*. Paper presented at PMI® Global Congress 2011—North America, Dallas, TX. Newtown Square, PA: Project Management Institute.

results. This is a method that I've used for many of my own projects, including starting a podcast and writing this book. It's a methodology that we actually broadly applied to a series of construction projects I worked on as well when I was working for the Air Force. We would prioritize a very select group of small renovation projects or maintenance projects to be quickly funded and implemented. The idea was that the projects could be managed in a very short amount of time, and the end result would be a large amount of accomplishments in a set period. These projects were my absolute favorite to work on because they moved so quickly and one project evolved into the next.

As a multi-passionate entrepreneur, this project sprint method aligns perfectly with that internal clock telling you when you've had enough of something. Once you figure out how long you're actually able to stick to doing work on a given subject before needing to move on, you can very easily apply that timeline to this scrum method of managing your work. For example, I know that after two to three months of working on one thing consistently, I tend to get bored and want to move on to the next thing. Therefore, I can use that timeframe to my advantage in planning my projects. I've been able to use two month or less projects to accomplish the goals that fall in line with my big picture vision.

Doing this allows you to prioritize the work that most inspires you and also what will give you the greatest amount of growth in your business. During these project periods, you want to focus on things that will allow you to move the needle and implement smaller pieces of your big vision. If that includes writing a book, like it did for me, then you may want to set aside two weeks to research and outline the book. Once you accomplish that, you may choose to push yourself to write the first two chapters in the next two weeks. The increments of time that work best for your own projects will be something that you've got to test out. You may find that you work best with two-week increments. Someone else may do better with a three-month sprint. You can test out a few projects at different lengths to see where your sweet spot lies, and then start applying this method to your bigger goals after you've figured out a good system. I do, however, encourage you to keep your timeframes as short as possible. Just know that the shorter the project timeline, the better your ability to get a quick win under your belt and build momentum for the next thing.

To be successful with this method, you've got to be able to prioritize the projects that will add up to the future vision that you want. Yes, you can move forward with any project here, but the idea is to be mindful about the ones that will actually take you in the direction you hope to eventually end up. Ask yourself what components make up the big picture vision you have for success. Do you intend to be a speaker, workshop host, or run a mastermind group? If so, then pull out the steps of each one of those things you want until you can identify manageable pieces starting to come to light.

For example, in order to be a speaker, you may need to start by giving small, free talks to local organizations. To do that, you could begin by doing a three-week project sprint to write a speech and pitch the topic to at least three local groups. If you were looking at the workshops component, you may decide that you could start by offering a weekend course at a local community college. In order to do that, you could set up a week long project sprint to communicate with the continuing education office of the college and outline a curriculum plan that suits them for the workshop.

Do you see how you can work backward and define smaller projects to get you to your bigger goal? You just have to be willing to look at the big picture as well as the individual components. That's the best way to make it all feel more manageable and like you have the ability to focus on your priorities at the moment. As long as you're moving in the right direction, you've got the ability to shift gears and work on different things. Just keep your focus through batching your time and defining clear projects that will get you to where you want to be.

––––––––––––––

When it comes to prioritizing, sometimes you need to listen to how you're feeling in the moment. If you originally planned to work on one thing, but then you feel really compelled to go in a different direction, listen to your gut. There's a reason you're feeling pulled that way so it's a good idea to follow that feeling and see where it

leads you. This is an essential part of being a multi-passionate entrepreneur. Although, I know for me, it's taken
a while to understand this. However, what I've learned
through all the trial and error is that you are the only
one who ultimately knows what works for you. You
know deep down what works for your lifestyle, the
projects that will light you up, and where you shine the
brightest. By working on what inspires you, you'll be
giving yourself the best use of your genius because
that's when you'll do your best work: when inspiration
strikes.

In the book, *Big Magic*, author Elizabeth Gilbert talks
about the idea of allowing your inspiration to guide
you.[103] She mentions that you never really know when
the inspiration for something is going to strike. It could
be in the middle of the night, or it could be when you're
supposed to be doing other things. However, you've got
to embrace those moments when you're feeling the
creative flow or when you've got a spark of an idea.
That's when the magic happens and messages start to
come through you that just have to get out into the
world, and it's your job to listen and relay those important messages and ideas. You're the one that's been
entrusted with the job of expressing them and presenting them through your unique viewpoint. So, allowing
yourself the space to accept that inspiration and be
grateful for it will allow further inspiration to flow freely

---

[103] Gilbert, Elizabeth. (2015). *Big Magic: Creative Living Beyond
Fear.* New York, New York: Riverhead Books.

as well.[104] That's such a powerful way to look at how you can listen to your inner voice and let that be your guide rather than just trying every tactic or business idea out there.

It's a balancing act, for sure, to be able to identify when you've got to stick something out and push through a project or when you need to listen to your inner compass and move on to what inspires you. That's why I advocate for those project sprints and the Scrum Method to give you flexibility. You want to create little micro-commitments for yourself so that you're able to actually accomplish things but at the same time instinctually let yourself be guided on the right path. Listen to inspiration when it strikes. Don't deny the ideas you have, but make decisions around how you choose to implement those ideas and when. Then, stick to the timeframe that you've chosen. If you get the urge to work on something else while you've already got a project in the works, then take the time to make notes for yourself and get all of your ideas out on paper. Recognizing and capturing your thoughts will allow you to release it from your mind for a little while so that you can focus on your project at hand and then come back to your new ideas with fresh eyes whenever the time is right.

Getting all of your thoughts down on paper can also help you to make a judgment call about whether it actu-

---

[104] Gilbert, Elizabeth. (2015). *Big Magic: Creative Living Beyond Fear*. New York, New York: Riverhead Books.

ally is a good time to switch gears and pursue it at that moment or if you need to just capture the idea for later. Sometimes if it's something big that would take you in a different direction, then you would want to pivot. My recommendation in this instance, though, would be to let that inspiration simmer for awhile after capturing the ideas. You don't want to get to a place where you've got shiny object syndrome, as we discussed in previous chapters, where you're being pulled to every new idea that comes to mind. The point of acknowledging your new, inspiring ideas is to give them their due bit of attention so that you continue to get inspiration. It's not that you should be abandoning your current projects in favor of a new one all the time. Rather, you've got to pay attention to those thoughts to see how they really fit into your vision before you choose to dive into them fully.

As you do more and more projects and move forward with establishing your business and your brand, you're going to want to include your growing audience in what you're working on at the moment. You may begin wondering what's the best way to share your work with them as you're working on it and how to give them glimpses into what you do behind the scenes. It's important to be open and honest with your community about why you're doing what you're doing. They may just see that you've been quiet on social media for awhile or that you've written a book one month and then hosting webinars the next. Because of this, your audience may not have a full understanding of exactly what it is that you're trying to achieve. That's why you need to let them in on your vision.

Giving them some insight into what you're trying to build for your business and how it helps them will not only help keep you accountable in diligently working to get there but also make your audience more invested in your work and vision as well. They'll be able to see the importance of the projects you're working on and how they fit together to give them better solutions or better experiences. Share why you've chosen to work on certain things. Talk about which parts of your work you've enjoyed and which parts have made a significant impact on your community. Give them some perspective on what's coming up and what the impact will be to them.

Every time you start a new project, work on a new product, or launch a new service, convey why it matters to your audience and how it fits into the big picture of your brand. If you're a jewelry designer, and you've got a new collection coming out, then show your customers how the new pieces will fill a gap in your product line and help them improve their look as well. If you use social media to communicate with your audience, take advantage of posting things like behind the scenes images, day-in-the-life videos, or sneak peeks to build interest in what will be coming down the pipeline for your brand. These are great ways to encourage engagement and turn your followers into fans invested in supporting your brand.

Keep in mind as you do this that you are the one that leads your tribe. No matter what you do, it's your job to help the people that follow you understand how everything you offer ties together. It may be obvious to you, but it won't be to them until you actually show them. In this way, storytelling can prove to be a huge asset to your business. You can use the power of sharing your stories, both from what you've learned and experienced as well as what you're going through now, to connect with your community. Stories are a great way to drive home a message for people because they'll connect what you're saying to an emotion. If you want to get them excited about what you're doing, then use a story to help them share in it right alongside you.

You're probably starting to identify how your experiences have shaped where you are in your life or business now. It may not seem like those things add up to a good story, but I bet for the people you're trying to reach, they do. No matter how eventful or how boring your life may seem to you, there's always someone else who can relate or learn from your same lessons and experience. That's why you should be using your story to show others what's achievable for them as well.

If you can tell one impactful story of your evolution to where you are now in a compelling way, then you'll be able to really resonate with your ideal customer on a much deeper level than if you were just trying to sell them something. This story of how you've gotten to where you are now is your brand story, and you should be using it throughout all of your content and marketing efforts. Your story is a prime way for your audience to get to know you, like you, and trust you right from the beginning and continue to do so the more they hear and resonate with that story themselves.

Okay, so what exactly would make your story compelling to someone? Well, basically, every good story has some type of conflict or pain point that shows what someone struggles with, a climax where everything essentially comes to a head, and a resolution to that conflict in the end, which is a way out of the continuous struggle and into a better place. Now, you might be thinking that you just want to help people do something simple like learning to cook, and there's no big struggle in that other than putting food on the table. You don't need to have some huge saga or dramatic sob story that was part of your life in order to get people to respond to your brand story. It just has to be a central component of what has gotten you to where you are now.

It could be as simple as you originally needing to figure out how to cook for your family of four and put dinner on the table every night. So after you could only take so much fast food every week, you decided to take a few cooking classes to learn the basics of healthy meals. Now, you're able to put dinner on the table in thirty minutes or less every night. You've got your problem, your climax, and your resolution. That's everything you need to tell a compelling story and relate to someone.

That example was very to-the-point, but that could easily work as a brand story if that were actually your struggle. Heartbreak, despair, and bankruptcy are not necessary here unless you actually have gone through those things. Otherwise, just share what's actually gotten you to the point where you are now. What has changed in your life for the better? And what can you help others to change as well? If you're a product-based business, then there's a reason you sell what you sell. You chose it to fill a gap in the market and provide some benefit to people. Share the story of how you came to be a product-based business owner and what that journey entailed for you leading up to the decision to open your shop.

This is not rocket science, but it does require a bit of sociology here in that you're tapping into how people respond to your brand and build a relationship with you as the founder of that brand. You've got to have an understanding of what it takes for someone to relate to you, trust you, and want to be part of your community. First and foremost, what can you say to your ideal customer that would make them think, "Wow, this person totally gets me! They've been where I am now and they've been able to turn things around and make improvements in their life. I want to do that, too!" What parts of your journey thus far could you share with someone to make them think that? It's not that you don't have anything compelling that's happened in your life.

It's probably that you just haven't figured out how to shape what you've gone through into a captivating story just yet.

Let's look at Martha Stewart's brand story as a well-known example. She grew up in a household of six children and learned a lot about maintaining a household including cooking, sewing, and gardening.[105] Throughout the years she studied architectural history, was a model, and even worked as a stockbroker. When she decided to leave her job on Wall Street during an economic downturn, things completely shifted for her. She turned to renovate the home she and her then-husband had purchased and started focusing more on cooking through teaching cooking classes and catering. After several years of running her own catering business, she wrote her first book, *Entertaining,* which really created a snowball effect for her career and set her up to become the massive household name that she is today.[106]

Looking at the Martha Stewart brand story, you can see that she started by being a multi-passionate person that didn't really know what she wanted to do. She tried many different avenues in her professional career. After

[105] Editors at Advameg, Inc. (2018). "Martha Stewart." Retrieved from https://www.referenceforbusiness.com/biography/S-Z/Stewart-Martha-1941.html
[106] Editors at Advameg, Inc. (2018). "Martha Stewart." Retrieved from https://www.referenceforbusiness.com/biography/S-Z/Stewart-Martha-1941.html

she struggled to make those work, she made the decision to go out on her own and be her own boss. She began tapping into her many talents and honing the skills she grew up learning. Then, Stewart was able to turn everything around and teach others how to create that same comforting lifestyle through cooking, crafting, and all things home-related.

Now, her story has a struggle, a pivot point, and a resolution. It conveys her drive and focus to succeed and how she was able to learn each of the skills that make up this crafty lifestyle surrounding her brand. Martha went through the steps of learning how to cook and sew, how to cater and throw parties, and all of the things that are part of her brand now so that she could give others the benefit of that same knowledge in order to live a comforting, homemade lifestyle as well.

You may have a very straightforward progression of how you got to where you are. You might have had a significant event trigger a change for you. You might just have decided one day that you had had enough and wanted to do things differently. No matter what your journey has been, there's always a progression. If you can hit on those major points of the progression with your struggle, climax or pivot point, and resolution, you'll be able to tell a compelling story of how it's all unfolded for you.

The most prominent components that your audience needs to resonate with are the pain point or struggle and the resolution. Do they feel the same now as you did during your struggle? Do they want to eventually reach the same outcome that you have reached? Do they wish they could achieve what you have achieved? If so, then you're probably a great match for that audience, and your story will hit home for them.

Action Exercise:

Now that you've got an understanding of how to develop a brand story, it's your turn to develop your own. First, give yourself some time to sit for at least ten minutes to gather your thoughts and outline your story. You want to lay out a timeline of what has happened in your life to bring you to the point where you are now. You can do this by working backward from the present if you find that easier, or you can start with the beginning at the time of your struggles or pain point. Draw out a line on your paper and delineate specific points along the line for each component of your story. The starting point should be somewhere around when you were struggling. The midpoint should cover one or multiple areas where you had a shift or change of some sort, and the endpoint should be where you are now or the end result that you've achieved.

Write down anything you specifically remember about what you were going through or where you were in your life in the beginning stages of your journey. Jot down notes about how you felt and what you were thinking at the time. What was it that you wanted when you were struggling? What was getting you through it? Then, move on to what happened in between. Were there any instances where you had insights into your situation? Did something happen to prompt you to make a change? Was there a point where you just couldn't take the status quo anymore? Write down any memories that come to mind and be sure to jot down the emotions that you felt in those moments as well.

Now, for the endpoint of your story timeline. This is where you are now that you've figured things out or made a change for the better. Write down exactly what is different now compared to the beginning and what you have to show for the change. What specifically was the result of your journey? What was the benefit of that change you made and how has it improved your life or business? Paint a picture when you describe what things look like now and add in the feelings associated with your current status.

Once you've taken the time to do that, you should have the major points of your story outlined. Now you just have to tie it all together with emotion, just like any good storyteller would. This is a bit like when you were a kid and you would tell ghost stories with friends late at night during a sleepover or campout. You would amp up the scariness factor and add in all kinds of details to make it extra scary so that you're friends would feel the intensity of the story, get scared, and clutch their pillows just waiting to hear what happened next. Well, not to that extreme, but you do want to add in some strong emotion to your story so that your audience can actually feel what you felt and empathize with you in those moments. The more enthralled you can get them, the better.

Remember to tell your story in a way that's authentic to you, though. Be genuine and real in order to get your point across. You don't have to over exaggerate. You just have to give it to people straight and be honest about what that meant for you as a person. People will respond because they've gone through the same thing and empathize with your feelings. If you try to over exaggerate, it'll just make your story less likely to hit home for someone. It'll start to feel more like an over the top ghost story rather than a real-life account. Just stick to your memory of how your experiences felt to you and your feelings about how much better things are now.

After you have your timeline down on paper, you want to write out your entire brand story so that you can see it in full and read it aloud. It takes some time to understand how the pieces all fit together and be able to clearly convey your journey. Chances are you're gonna fall into one of these categories: 1. It's all jumbled up in your mind, and you need to get it to a point where it all makes sense together to get your point across, 2. You've got too many gaps in your timeline and need to fill it in with more milestones to get it to make sense, or 3. You've got so much that you want to convey that you need to refine your ideas down to just the key points in your story that really delineate the change that has occurred in your life.

Whichever group you fall into, you can benefit from taking your timeline story and writing it out into paragraphs by connecting the memories together and linking them to emotions. Then, once you've got it all written out as one congruent story, you need to read it aloud at least two or three times. I know this is a step that you're most likely to skip, but in all honesty, it's a really important one. You can't understand how your story actually sounds to someone or how it will come across until you actually hear it out loud. Things sound entirely different when you hear them versus when you read them.

This is actually something I'm learning over again as I write this book because part of a thorough editing process is to read your book aloud. That way, you'll hear how it sounds and be able to catch so many more things that need to be fixed than if you had just written it out and read it in your head. So you'll want to read it aloud a few times and see how it flows. On top of being able to fill in the gaps where things don't make sense, this will also give you the opportunity to practice telling your story. After all, you're not just going to always be writing it out in copy. You're also going to be recounting it on video during webinars, live videos for your audience, interviews, podcasts, or any other ways that you communicate with your audience.

Your story will become something that you reference on a regular basis to get your message across and to get new people who have never interacted with you before to understand what you're all about. In this way, owning your story and knowing exactly what points are important to drive home and which emotions are critical to convey will give you an advantage when it comes to connecting with your ideal customers as soon as they come across your brand. This is how you stand out to someone in the first few seconds of them finding you, and it's also how you keep them coming back to work with you.

One last thing to note here is that utilizing your story to connect with your tribe doesn't stop after they see you that first time and hear your brand story. It continues in all of your content as you want to regularly show them the benefit and the value of working with you and being part of your brand. You want to show them that the thing they want to achieve, that you and your audience both values, is accessible to them and that you can lead them to that. To do this, you show your story in your photos, you talk about it in your videos, and you link to articles associated with what you value. Your content embodies the end result of your journey: the ideal outcome for your audience.

That's a powerful thing if you can harness your story and carry it through in all of your branding and marketing efforts. You'll be well on your way to establishing a strong connection with your audience and building that trust in what you do. Little by little, you can do this by planning out ways to incorporate your brand story into your business. You don't have to do it all overnight, but if you can at least start to emphasize the journey you've been on and how it's relevant to your audience, you'll put yourself in a much better spot over time.

Let's take this all back full circle to your core driving message. That should always be the central focus of all that you do. So invest your time into projects that will spread that message or support it in some way. The path you take to lead your audience to what they value needs to always have your core message as the navigator. It's the thing that steers the ship and the thing that allows you to keep blinders on to everything else that may be a distraction. If something doesn't fit into your core message, get rid of it or pursue it in your personal time instead.

When you're putting together a path that leads to an end goal, keep in mind that it's not just about your own end goal here. It's most importantly about the result for your community. That is, it's the thing that you are leading them to on the other side of the river where they want to be. Thus, you should be creating stepping stones for them to get across that river and make it to what they value most on the other side. The projects you choose to do need to relate not only to your core message but also to your customer's journey. They need to get them closer and closer to that end goal. Therefore, you need to be continually asking yourself how what you're doing is helping them to progress. Will you help them solve a big part of their problem when they read your book? Will you provide support for them in a coaching program? How are you showing up to serve them in their journey to what they want to achieve? Your business isn't only about you or what you want to do. It's about putting their needs first. Knowing exactly how your projects will benefit your customers gives them a much higher likelihood of being well-received by your community and in turn making an impact.

Many experts will tell you that when you're testing things out and putting new work out into the world, you should fail fast. Essentially, they're telling you to take action and see what works as quickly as possible. If something doesn't stick, then move on to trying something else as fast as possible. In this way, you're not spinning your wheels planning or thinking about the perfect scenario, just as we discussed in previous chapters. Your ability to fail fast and pivot to the next thing will be the difference between being forever stuck and unsure of what direction to take and growing a successful business that serves your community well. You've got to embrace failure and recognize it as a sign that you're taking action and constantly learning. The good thing for you as a multi-passionate entrepreneur is that you most likely learn quite quickly and don't have any issue with moving on to the next thing. Use that to your advantage here when you're working on different projects in the beginning and figuring out what works and what doesn't.

For myself, I've tested out so many different business ventures over the years. Every time I realize something doesn't fit, I understand myself or who I want to serve a little bit better, and that's when I pivot. To outsiders, this may seem like you're just constantly quitting and starting over again. Yet, in reality, you're learning what's right for you and your ideal audience and making adjustments to keep you on track toward your goals.

Keep in mind that the important part is not how you get to your goals. As long as you get clear about what you want and work diligently to head in that direction, you'll find your way. We all would like to take the straightest path possible, but sometimes that's not what we really need in our lives. Sometimes we're meant to take a winding, hilly road that leads us all over the map before we get to our destination. Instead of getting frustrated over this, tell yourself again and again that how you get there is not the important part. Learning to let go and enjoy the ride is what will make doing all of this worth it in the long run.

Sticking to any initial decisions you make isn't required. Flexibility is your best friend here, and giving yourself grace in the process is one of the best things you can do to take care of yourself through it all. You are in the process of living your purpose as you share your gifts and talents. By honoring all that you are, you're putting your light out into the world and making it a better place. If starting a business is about creating something that will give you fulfillment, then look no further than to utilize what's inside of you right now. None of the latest strategies will be as powerful as that. You've got everything you need within you already, and it's waiting for you to tap into it. Get out of your own way, start listening to your inner compass, and let that be your guide to creating a business you love through your unique potential. Your big vision is waiting and so are your people.

No Niche Necessary

Download your FREE audiobook of

No Niche Necessary

at:

www.kristenleighking.com/NoNicheNecessary-
Audiobook

**Your passions are waiting!
I can't wait to see how you share them and make an
impact in the world.**

Kristen

About the Author

Kristen Leigh King is a former military officer and architectural project manager turned designer, photographer and brand strategist for creative entrepreneurs. As a self-proclaimed "creative anthropologist," she finds expressive ways to explore the way people live and work. Over the years, she has discovered what it takes to grow as a multi-passionate entrepreneur by leading from within. Kristen emphasizes the importance of incorporating who you are and what you stand for into creating a cohesive, multi-passionate brand. By coupling her experience in both practical and creative fields, she helps other entrepreneurs bring their visions to fruition and step into the impactful role they're meant to assume.

**Find more from the author at:
www.kristenleighking.com**